Kierkegaard's Socratic Art

T0204414

Kierkegaard's Socratic Art

by
Benjamin Daise

MERCER UNIVERSITY PRESS
1979 · 1999
Twenty Years of Publishing Excellence

ISBN 0-86554-655-X   MUP/P195

Library of Congress Cataloging-in-Publication Data

Daise, Benjamin.
    Kierkegaard's socratic art / by Benjamin Daise. — 1st ed.
    p. cm.
    Includes bibliographical references and index.
    ISBN 0-86554-655-X (alk. paper).
        1. Kierkegaard, Søren, 1813–1855—Authorship. I. Title.

B4378.P74 D35 1999
198'.9 21; aa05 09-21—dc99

                                               99-048303

Contents

to Laurel

Preface

The thesis for which this book offers support is Søren Kierkegaard's claim that Christendom needed a midwife and that he knew how to be one.

> One can now do with me what one will, insult me, envy me stop reading me, beat me, kill me: that which one cannot in all eternity deny, which was my idea and my life, that it is one of the most original thoughts in a long time and the most original in the Danish language: that Christendom needed a midwife and I understood being that—while no one understood appreciating it. (P VIII 1A 42)

The "midwife" metaphor is clearly a reference to Socrates, since Socrates referred to himself as a midwife (see *Theaetetus* 149a-150e). "Christendom" refers to the officially Christian status of Denmark. Kierkegaard distinguishes the cultural phenomenon (*Christendom*) from the genuine coin, Christianity (*Christenhed*). The remark is to be understood, then, as a claim Kierkegaard makes about the relationship between himself and his culture. This includes Kierkegaard's understanding about the relationship between his authorship and his culture.

In chapter 1, I attempt to clarify just what characteristics Kierkegaard has in mind when he refers to himself as a midwife for Christendom. I do this by taking an example of Socrates at work in one of Plato's dialogues. In Plato's *Meno*, Socrates employs a number of strategies that exemplify his role as gadfly in Athens. By paying close attention to what transpires in that work, we are able to see what it is important to attend to in order, first, to avoid misunderstanding the text, and, then, to reach some understanding of the text. We will see, among other things, the importance of refusing to yield to the philosopher's impulse to assign a thesis.

Additionally, I consider the question of just how we are to understand what Kierkegaard calls "indirect communication." How exactly might it be distinguished from other communication? What is the rationale for its use? Kierkegaard offers two kinds of justification for indirect communication. One kind may be seen as pragmatic. The other, an ethical justification, is suggested but is not developed.

As I said, what I offer is support for a claim that is Kierkegaard's, and that means that the thesis in question has been around for as long as Kierkegaard's works. Indeed, Kierkegaard himself made the notion of "indirect communication" a category for independent study. Closer to home, Louis Mackey, to whom I am indebted for my sense of the spirit in which to read Kierkegaard, has argued eloquently for seeing Kierkegaard as something other than a traditional kind of philosopher. He provided a reading of some texts to exhibit the sense in which Kierkegaard might be understood as "a kind of poet."

In spite of Mackey's work, Kierkegaard is still treated in many quarters as a traditional kind of philosopher. Prior to Mackey's book, Brand Blanshard ascribed to Kierkegaard the thesis that "[t]he final step [in life's stages] is a passionate, nonrational 'leap of faith,' a commitment of feeling and will. What is the commitment to? Not to a way of life merely, as some readers have supposed, but also to Christian belief. And the central Christian belief, he holds, is belief in the incarnation."[1] In the same year as Mackey's book, Paul Edwards wrote that "[t]he doctrine that 'may well have marked a turning point in European philosophy' is Kierkegaard's theory identifying truth with 'subjectivity.' "[2] In *The Logic of Subjectivity*, Louis Pojman deals with indirect communication in an appendix, after having constructed arguments he sees in the Climacian works that aim at providing a rational justification for Christianity.[3] In his *Kierkegaard's "Fragments" and "Postscript,"* Stephen Evans rightly notes that it is a mistake simply to identify the views of the pseudonyms with Kierkegaard's views as well as a mistake to rule out Kierkegaard's agreeing with some things said

---

[1]Brand Blanshard, "Kierkegaard on Faith," *The Personalist* 49 (1968): 5.

[2]Paul Edwards, "Kierkegaard and the 'Truth' of Christianity," *Philosophy* 46/176 (April 1971): 89.

[3]Louis Pojman, *The Logic of Subjectivity* (University AL: University of Alabama Press, 1984) 132.

by his pseudonyms.[4] I would note that honoring indirect communication is not just a matter of accurate attribution of views. Evans is certainly sensitive to that when, for example, in *Passionate Reason* in 1992, he addresses Climacus's motivation for denying the relevance of historical evidence to faith.[5] (It will be seen that I dispute Evans's account of the motivation.) Still, understanding the works as indirect communication takes more than an occasional reference to the motivation of the pseudonymous authors. The clearest and most recent example of my point is Wilfried Greve's challenge to reading Kierkegaard as indirect communication. With particular reference to *Fear and Trembling*, of all things, he says:

> First there remain some open questions concerning such a type of interpretation: Why should it be allowed to deny a theoretical discussion (like de Silentio's discussion of the moral-religion problem) any value of its own? And why do we have to take exactly this part of the Kierkegaardian work as allegorical or symbolic? What about the other parts? At least there is missing a justification for such a reading of Kierkegaard anyhow.[6]

As Greve's remarks suggest, the reason for taking Kierkegaard as a traditional philosopher may be that there are so many sentences in the works that look for all the world like bits of philosophy. Take, for example, the following: "Immediate sensation and immediate cognition cannot deceive."[7] How could that be anything but a piece of a discourse on epistemology? In short, the problem seems to be that any defense of the thesis I support that does not provide an account of how the particular philosophical-sounding claims play a role in an other than traditional philosophical enterprise may leave those inclined to treat Kierkegaard as a traditional

---

[4]C. Stephen Evans, *Kierkegaard's "Fragments" and "Postscript,": The Religious Philosophy of Johannes Climacus* (Highlands NJ: Humanities Press, 1983) 7-8.

[5]C. Stephen Evans, *Passionate Reason: Making Sense of Kierkegaard's "Philosophical Fragments"* (Bloomington: Indiana University Press, 1992) 159.

[6]Wilfried Greve, "Against Authority: Abraham in Kierkegaard Research," 9, a paper presented at the International Kierkegaard Conference, St. Olaf College, 11 June 1997.

[7]Kierkegaard, *Philosophical Fragments*, trans. Howard V. Hong and Edna H. Hong (Princeton NJ: Princeton University Press, 1985) 81.

philosopher unconvinced. Greve's challenge needs to be met not just on a case by case basis, but for the pseudonymous authorship.

In chapter 2, I offer detailed textual analysis of the questions that are explicitly addressed in *Philosophical Fragments*, in order to show that what are ostensibly traditional metaphysical and epistemological issues are not those kinds of questions at all and that the formulation of the questions is demanded by the maieutic requirements of the environment in which Kierkegaard wrote. Kierkegaard had to deal in the linguistic currency of the day, but he was not simply bound by that currency. I show how Socratic maneuvers allow *Fragments* to be responsive to the questions it poses in a way that is not limited by the assumptions of the day.

In chapter 3, I directly confront interpretations of the Climacian writings that see Climacus as presenting traditional kinds of responses to theological or metaphysical questions. It is necessary for me to provide some criticism of plausible accounts of portions of *Fragments* and *Postscript* that see Climacus as holding the kind of view I deny that he holds. I do this as part of an effort to provide analysis of textual language that shows the concern of Climacus to be *wholly* existential in character, not just *primarily* existential.

As I indicated, Kierkegaard hints at, but does not develop an ethical justification for indirect communication. Thus, finally, in chapter 4, I examine possible arguments for the ethical requirement of indirect communication by Kierkegaard in order to assess Kierkegaard's claim.

Chapter 1

Indirect Communication

Socratic Art in Meno

In Plato's *Meno*, the arguments about whether or not virtue is teachable play a crucial role in the strategy of Socrates. There are two arguments that end with conflicting conclusions. The first one ends with the conclusion that virtue can be taught. The second one ends with the conclusion that virtue cannot be taught. The conflict is left unresolved in the dialogue. That fact is understandable if what transpires is seen as the manifestation of a strategy that I refer to as the "Socratic art." If we see how the arguments function, we will see what the Socratic art involves. We will see that what is involved is not just a matter of asking and answering questions. Nor is it just a matter of constructing and examining arguments for competing answers. Neither is it just refutation through cross-examination or any combination of the maneuvers just mentioned. The strategy also involves the kind of role-playing that allows the positions taken and the arguments made to be seen as cultural representatives. Consequently, the figure of Socrates can be seen as functioning as a *dramatis persona*, one that embodies the Athenian conflict about the nature of virtue. Since the arguments in question are made in the second half of the dialogue, some setting of the stage for them is necessary.

Preliminary Maneuvers

Unlike other Platonic dialogues, *Meno* opens abruptly, without any dramatic introduction. Meno asks Socrates, "Can you tell me, Socrates, can virtue be taught? Or is it not teachable but the result of practice, or is it neither of these, but men possess it by nature or in some other way?" (*Meno* 70a). Meno's posing of questions outside any lived context in which they might naturally arise suggests to us that the questions do not grow out of any genuine concerns that Meno has. Socrates' ironic response in which he says that he and other Athenians claim no knowledge of virtue shows that he reads *Meno* in the same way. Socrates makes it clear that he thinks Meno is simply in the habit, acquired through the influence of the Sophist, Gorgias, of hearing and giving confidently delivered speeches on any topic whatsoever and that Meno is trying to stimulate some such response from Socrates. The immediate problem faced by Socrates, then, is Meno himself. Meno is not disposed towards any inquiry about virtue, because he thinks he knows what there is to know about it, and complete knowledge, real or imagined, is an unfailing impediment to inquiry. If Socrates is to engage Meno in inquiry, he must get Meno to ask his questions seriously, and if he is to get Meno to do that, Meno must be chastened and, thereby, changed. The immediate objective of this approach is explicitly discussed in Sophist as one of eradicating "the spirit of conceit" (*Sophist* 230a).

The problem of Meno's character is only one problem for Socrates. The other problem is Meno's lack of understanding of the proper procedure for inquiry. There are some questions that are logically prior to others, and if the order of inquiry is not respected, one cannot expect to prosper intellectually. Meno has raised a question about what attributes to ascribe to something without first identifying the something. "If I do not know what something is," Socrates asks, "how could I know what qualities it possesses?" (*Meno* 71b).

Socrates' profession of ignorance serves a double purpose. (1) It serves as the basis for enticing Meno into saying what he thinks virtue is. This initiates the Socratic elenchus that culminates in Meno's being chastened. Every effort made by Meno to say what virtue is meets with disaster in the form of Socrates' questions, and Meno is duly chastened. Thus is part of the first problem faced by Socrates addressed. (2) The profession of ignorance about what virtue is also focusses attention on the question that is logically prior to the one asked by Meno. In that way, the intellectual problem is also addressed.

The first part of the strategy works perhaps too well, since Meno becomes frustrated and combative and raises doubts about the possibility of inquiry with the noted "eristic dilemma."

> But how will you look for something when you don't know
> anything at all (*parapan*) about it? How are you going to set up
> something as the object of your search? To put it another way,
> even if you come right up against it, how will you know that
> what you have found is the thing you didn't know? (*Meno* 80d)

The move is clearly a psychologically defensive one. Meno is
attempting to ascribe the blame for his failure to the enterprise
itself rather than to any shortcoming on his part. That attitude is
as inimical to the possibility of inquiry as Meno's initial stance. It
calls, however, for a different strategy. Socrates' response this time
is to try to smooth Meno's ruffled feathers by telling a hopeful
story in the way one might do to coax a pouting child out of his
or her obstinacy. Before he tells the story, Socrates formulates
Meno's series of rhetorical questions as an argument.

> Do you realize that what you are bringing up is the eristic
> argument that a person cannot try to discover what he knows or
> does not know? He would not seek for what he knows, for since
> he knows it there is no need for inquiry, nor what he does not
> know, for in that case he does not even know what to look for.
> (*Meno* 80e)

As Julius Moravcsik points out, this argument is not the one that
is strictly derivable from Meno's questions, for it leaves out the
qualification "anything at all" (*parapan*).[1] Michael Welbourne dis-
agrees with Moravcsik about the significance of the omission.
According to him, the questions posed by Meno constitute a problem for Socrates, since Socrates had expressed utter ignorance of
virtue and the solution offered in the recollection story "is not
tailored to fit the eristic restatement."[2] It is designed to undercut
Socrates' claim of complete ignorance.

Now, whatever one may think of the status of Socrates' claims
of ignorance in general, surely the claim at *Meno* 71b that is cited
by Welbourne is not to be taken literally. It is made in conjunction
with the claim that every Athenian would make the same profession of ignorance, and it follows the attribution of a philosophical

---

[1]Julius Moravcsik, "Learning as Recollection," in *Plato*, ed. Gregory Vlastos
(Garden City NY: Doubleday, 1971) 1:57.

[2]Michael Welbourne, "*Meno*'s Paradox," *Philosophy* 61 (1986): 238.

bent to Meno and other Thessalians. There could not be clearer signs of nonliteralness. In *Crito*, Socrates refers to Thessaly as "the home of indiscipline and laxity" (*Crito* 53d). Given that, it would make absolutely no sense for Plato to fashion a response to a literal understanding of the remark. For us, there is a relatively easy solution to the "dilemma" posed by Meno. That is the significance of the observation by Moravcsik. It points to the difference between a sound but irrelevant argument and an unsound argument. The following simple argument is the one that might be made on the basis of Meno's rhetorical question. (Discovery = Success in seeking [not accidental finding].)

1. If X does not know (at all) Y, then X cannot seek Y.
2. (Assume) X does not know (at all) Y.
3. Therefore, X cannot seek Y.
4. If X cannot seek Y, then X cannot discover Y.
5. Therefore, X cannot discover Y.

This argument is a sound one, but it is utterly irrelevant to inquiry, since inquiry does not presuppose utter ignorance. The argument that might be formulated on the basis of Socrates' restatement of Meno's position is a bit more complex.

(1) Either X knows Y or X does not know Y.
     Assume X knows Y.
(2) If X knows Y, X has no reason to seek Y.
(3) If X has no reason to seek Y, X will not seek Y.
(4) If X does not seek Y, X cannot discover Y.
(5) Therefore, X cannot discover Y.
     Assume X does not know Y
(2*) If X seeks Y, then Y is the object of X's search.
(3*) If Y is the object of X's search, then X knows Y.
     But by hypothesis
(4*) X does not know Y.
(5*) Therefore, Y is not the object of X's search.
(6*) Therefore, X does not seek Y.
(7*) If X does not seek Y, X cannot discover Y.
(8*) Therefore, X cannot discover Y.

Now, if we understand "knowing" to mean "knowing altogether" (*parapan*) in the sense of having complete conceptual clarity and having all of the facts, then the first part of the argument (1 through 5) is sound but irrelevant to any human situation. But on that understanding, premise (3*) is just false. There is, of course, a sense of "knowing" in which premise (3*) is true. That is the sense in which knowing means "having some concept" (understanding) or "having some awareness." On that understanding, the movement from (4*) to (5*) is fallacious. The eristic dilemma is a "trick argument" because it trades on the ambiguity of "knowing." The argument is only relevant to inquiry when "knowing" is not understood as "knowing-*parapan*," but then it is unsound.

An explanation of the ambiguity accounts for the falsity of premise (3*), and that would have defused the dilemma. Moravcsik points out that there is no evidence for Plato's having the conceptual tools for doing that until *Sophist*.[3] However, the omission of *parapan* in the reformulation of Meno's argument points to an awareness of the significance of it. That omission is particularly noteworthy when we take into account the fact that Socrates had indicated his awareness of its importance by an earlier remark. "Do you think," he had asked Meno, "that someone who does not know Meno at all (*parapan*) could say whether he is handsome and rich and wellborn or the reverse?" (*Meno* 71b) While in this case, "knowledge of acquaintance" (*gignoskei*) is used and in Meno's question "knowledge that" (*oistha*) is used, the implication is the same: from utter ignorance, nothing. Also, with complete knowledge nothing, because there is no need of anything. This truth is the eristic dilemma as presented by Meno. It is, however, completely irrelevant to anything having to do with inquiry, because no one ever asks a question in utter ignorance. Socrates' reformulation of the argument without the qualification of ignorance as complete is an indication that he knows this and that the argument could have been addressed directly. His refusal to address directly even the reformulated argument indicates that he knows that the argument in whatever form it is made is not the immediate problem. The immediate problem is Meno's defensiveness. It is Meno himself.

The story of recollection, told in response to this situation, is not primarily an attempt to show that the argument legitimately attributable to Meno or the one formulated by Socrates is unsound. Indeed, it is not primarily an intellectual appeal at all. It is, rather,

---

[3]Moravcsik, "Learning as Recollection," 55.

an attempt to secure Meno's complicity in inquiry by changing his attitude. If Socrates' questioning has succeeded in its immediate objective of eradicating "the spirit of conceit," the explicitly stated aim of the elenchus, it has not succeeded in its further objective of replacing that spirit with a disposition to inquire. As Richard Robinson has pointed out, sometimes the elenchus produces anger and hostility, instead of the desired stimulus to inquiry.[4] According to Robinson, the disappearance of the stinging irony from the post-Socratic dialogues may be viewed as Plato's acknowledgement of the potential counterproductive effects of the elenchus. However, as Robinson says, Plato is aware of this possibility as early as *Apology* and Meno's posing of the eristic dilemma is certainly an acknowledgement of the fact that the elenchus alone was not always sufficient. The recollection story and along with it the slave-boy demonstration are the additional tools in Socrates' artistic repertoire aimed at winning Meno over.

In the demonstration, after an early success in answering a question in geometry, the boy thinks he can answer any question. He gives a wrong answer and is frustrated but is able to follow Socrates' questioning to the right answer. Socrates makes the parallel between Meno and the boy explicit.

> You realize, Meno, what point he has reached in his recollection. At first he did not know what the basic line of the eight-foot square was; even now he does not yet know, but then he thought he knew, and answered confidently as if he did know, and he did not think himself at a loss, but now he does think himself at a loss, and as he does not know, neither does he think he knows.
> . . .
> So isn't he now in a better position with regard to the matter he does not know? (*Meno* 84a-b)

Meno agrees. He is shown himself in someone else and is brought to see that it is better to admit ignorance and then to inquire than to cling stubbornly to the unfounded presumption of knowledge.

---

[4]Richard Robinson, *Plato's Earlier Dialectic* (Ithaca NY: Cornell University Press, 1941) 12-19.

He is, thus, placated and the first problem faced by Socrates, that of Meno's character, is at least temporarily solved.[5]

I have argued that the appeal made by the recollection story and slave boy demonstration is not *primarily* an intellectual appeal. Is it nonetheless *also* an intellectual appeal? Certainly, the effort makes some intellectual demands. It attempts to show that inquiry is possible by presenting a case of actual inquiry. So, the intellectual demand made on Meno at that point is only that he be able to infer the possibility from the actuality. Is the effort also an attempt to show *how* inquiry is possible? That is, is recollection presented as a theory of knowledge?

A full accounting of the place of recollection in Plato's thinking is beyond the scope of this inquiry. There is no doubt that in other places recollection takes on theoretical significance. In *Meno*, however, we are pointed away from that. (1) The story and demonstration are bracketed by disclaimers. Socrates attributes the story to "men and women who understand the truths of religion . . . " (*Meno* 81a) before he tells it. At the end of the demonstration, he says, "I shouldn't like to take my oath on the whole story . . . " (*Meno* 86b). (2) Late in the dialogue, recollection is completely demythologized. "[T]hey [true opinion] are not worth much until you tether them by working out the reason. That process . . . is recollection, as we agreed earlier" (*Meno* 96e). (3) The process encountered earlier, the slave boy demonstration, has a very mundane explanation, of which Socrates seems aware. The process that Socrates called recollecting, consisted in questions and answers establishing that the answer to the puzzle they were trying to solve was not four, because four was too large. Three was also too large. Two was too small. The answer must, therefore, be between two and three. A line called the diagonal, between two and three, was seen to fit the bill. What was needed, then, was the ability to wield the key concepts: *four, three, two, too large, too small, between.* And Socrates had established that beforehand by an apparently innocuous question. "He is Greek and speaks our language?" (*Meno* 82b) he asked. That is the prior knowledge (acquired in this

[5]Cf. R. S. Brumbaugh, "Plato's *Meno* as Form and as Content of Secondary School Courses in Philosophy," *Teaching Philosophy* 1/2 (Fall 1975): 111.

life) that is exploited in the process and the question points us to it. So, while there are good reasons for seeing the recollection story and slave boy demonstration as not having significant intellectual appeal, there is nonetheless an intellectual problem involved.

The Virtue Is Teachable Argument

While progress has been made on the first problem, the dialogue makes clear that the second one is still there, because Meno asks the same question with which the work began. The importance of the first Socratic maneuvers is underscored by the difference in tone and substance of Socrates' response this time. Socrates now has before him the kind of character, if not the kind of intellect, with whom inquiry is possible. He adopts a procedure appropriate for the situation. He decides to proceed "by means of a hypothesis" (*Meno* 86e). The hypothesis and the argument making use of it are as follows.

Hypothesis: If virtue is knowledge (*episteme*), then virtue is teachable. (87c) If virtue is not knowledge, then virtue is not teachable. (87c) That is, virtue is teachable if and only if it is knowledge.[6]

---

[6]A long line of commentators, including R. S. Bluck in *Plato's Meno*, p. 17, have identified the hypothesis as "Virtue is knowledge." Zyskind and Sternfeld indicate why that is. "The basic evidence is the concluding passage in which *Meno* summarizes the argument. The common reading is: 'and plainly, Socrates, on our hypothesis that virtue is knowledge, it must be taught' " (89C). (Harold Zyskind & R. Sternfeld, "Plato's *Meno* 89c: 'Virtue Is Knowledge,' a Hypothesis?" *Phronesis* 21/2: 131.) They argue, in agreement with Bluck, that the passage should be translated "and it is plain, Socrates, on the hypothesis, since virtue is knowledge, that it is teachable" (131). They say, then, that "[l]ogically this hypothesis is 'knowledge alone is teachable' " and proceed to show how the hypothetical statement that is used in the argument is derivable from it. My claim is that there is no need to go the route of derivation, since the example Socrates gives when he first mentions the method of hypothesis makes clear what it would take for the hypothesis to be true, and he follows that up with statements and questions to which the clear answers are statements that would be in the form exemplified. Those statements include the hypothetical one that is used in the argument.

The relevant passages are as follows. "When they are asked, for example, about a given area, whether it is possible for this area to be inscribed as a triangle in a given circle, they will probably reply: I don't know yet whether it fulfills the conditions, but I think I have a hypothesis which will help us in the matter. It is

1. If anything is virtue, it is good (87d).
2. If virtue is good, it is beneficial (87e).
3. If virtue is beneficial, it is wisdom (*phronesis*) (88c-d).
4. If anything is virtue, it is wisdom (88c-d, 89a).
   (Def. Wisdom is a kind of knowledge.)
5. If anything is virtue, it is knowledge.
6. If anything is virtue it is teachable (89c).

It is important to see that this argument reflects Athenian thinking about virtue. Since the term that is translated as virtue, *arete*, means "excellence," the first premise is tautologous. The connection between what is good and what is beneficial is almost as tightly made in Athenian thinking as the preceding connection. But somewhere between the two premises, the connection between being virtue and being beneficial is subject to some unravelling. In *Republic*, it is only as a last resort in the face of Socrates' criticism of his thesis that justice is the interest of the stronger does Thrasymachus say that he thinks it is injustice, not justice that is beneficial (*Republic* 343b-344c). Thrasymachus's explanation of his position is that it is the enlightened view in contrast to the naive one held by the masses who are under the control of leaders who want them to think exactly as they do. Thus, it appears that the first two premises of the argument reflect Athenian thinking but that they are not universally held nor, perhaps, very deeply held.

The third premise depends, in part, on something stated conditionally about the sort of thing that virtue is. "*If* virtue is something in the soul that must be beneficial, it must be wisdom" (*Meno* 88c; my emphasis). The assumption that virtue is something

---

this. *If* the area is such that, when one has applied it to the given line of the circle, it is deficient by another rectangle similar to the one which is applied, then, I should say, one result follows; *if not*, the result is different" (87 a; emphases mine). The hypothesis clearly has two parts, an if-then part and an if-not-then-not part, that are equivalent to if-and-only-if. The method is then applied to virtue. "Well, in the first place, if it [virtue] is anything but knowledge, is there a possibility of anyone teaching it . . . ? Isn't it plain to everyone that a man is not taught anything except knowledge" (87b-d). That is to say, if virtue is not knowledge, then it is not teachable. "If, on the other hand, virtue is some sort of knowledge, clearly it could be taught" (87c). Thus, the hypothesis clearly has two parts, even though it is only the last part presented that plays a role in the argument.

in the soul was made in formulating the question to which the hypothesis was a response. "What kind of thing *in the soul* must virtue be for it to be teachable or not?" (*Meno* 87b; my emphasis). This assumption limits the candidates for consideration for being virtue to a few acknowledged beneficial attributes of the soul, "justice, courage, intelligence, memory, generosity, and so on" (*Meno* 88b). This list can then be considered to see if there is anything on it that is different from knowledge and which would be beneficial in the absence of knowledge. This procedure that is used to rule out everything but wisdom, knowledge of how to use everything else sensibly, is explicitly dependent on the assumption that virtue is something in the soul. This assumption is one that is reflective of Athenian thinking.

The Virtue Is Not Teachable Argument

There is no hint given of any reason for thinking that there is anything wrong with the argument. Yet the conclusion is immediately challenged on the basis of the argument that follows. That argument is prefaced by the statement that it is not the hypothesis that is being challenged. "I do not withdraw the statement that if it is knowledge, it is teachable; but as for its being knowledge, consider if you think I have grounds for misgiving" (*Meno* 89d). The argument:

1. If anything is teachable, there are students and teachers of it (89d).
2. There are no students and teachers of virtue (96c).
3. Virtue is not teachable (96c).

Why would Plato have Socrates make this argument at this point? After all, it would seem that the objective has been achieved, since Meno agrees that virtue is teachable. Two closely related suggestions are that the argument is sound but limited in scope and that it is intentionally fallacious. Daniel Devereux claims that the argument is directed only against the possibility of teaching virtue when teaching is understood in the way the Sophists understood it, as transmission of knowledge from one person to another. "This argument," he says, "is therefore not at odds with the thesis that knowledge is a sufficient condition for virtue."[7] J. T. Bedu-Addo sees the argument as intentionally fallacious but as having the serious purpose of demonstrating the instability of true opinion. It would be sheer "sophistry" for Socrates to argue that true opinion, not knowledge is the useful guide in political conduct, he says. "Plato means the reader to see that the view that virtue is true opinion and not knowledge does not really make sense in the context of this dialogue."[8]

The problem with the first view is that there is no apparent reason for Socrates to invoke the Sophistic view of teaching at this point. What exactly is to be gained by showing that *on the Sophistic view of teaching*, virtue cannot be taught? There simply is not anything to motivate such a move. The problem with the second view is that no fallacy in the argument is identified and, indeed, the form of the argument is clearly a valid one.

The Arguments as Art

Now, what *is* problematic at this point in the dialogue is the identity of virtue and Meno's lack of knowledge about it. The first argument simply assumed that virtue is something in the soul. Just as in the beginning of the dialogue a strategy was contrived to focus attention on the need to ascertain what virtue is, the argument against the teachability of virtue is a device for doing the same thing. That is, while Meno seems to have followed the argument that virtue is teachable, there is no indication that he has been disabused of the view of virtue with which he began. That view of virtue is in conflict with the assumption operating in the argument from a hypothesis. (I will show this momentarily when I look more closely at the argument.) This is the kind of situation for which the elenchus is tailor-made. However, here is a situation in which that would not be the appropriate strategy, because it has already been used and Meno has felt its chastening force. Yet Meno does not feel the conflict that lives in him.

This unfelt conflict of Meno's is at the same time an Athenian conflict. The way Plato makes that point is by associating it with

---

[7]Daniel Devereux, "Nature and Teaching in Plato's *Meno*," *Phronesis* 23/2 (1978): 123.

[8]J. T. Bedu-Addo, "Recollection and the Argument from a Hypothesis in Plato's *Meno*," *Journal of Hellenic Studies* 104 (1984): 12.

Anytus, who was "brought up . . . well and . . . properly educated, as the Athenian people appreciate: look how they elect him into the highest offices in the state" (*Meno* 90b). Anytus is representative. He is also likened to the prechastened Meno by having him pronounce judgment on the Sophists with "no experience of them at all (*parapan*)" (*Meno* 92c). Further, he accepts the conclusion of the first argument, that virtue can be taught. Thus, the conflict produced by the second argument is his, too. Like the earlier Meno, he responds to Socrates' criticism with anger and hostility (*Meno* 95a).

The second argument is constructed by using the common view of virtue to identify would-be teachers of virtue. Anytus's view is that any Athenian gentleman can teach virtue. Socrates' selection of Pericles, Themistocles, Thucydides, and Aristides amounts to a best case scenario for Anytus. If any Athenian gentleman will do, then surely those who are preeminent among Athenian gentlemen will do. Premise #2, that there are no teachers and students of virtue, is made after considering that none of those mentioned was able to teach virtue to their sons.

The identification of the preeminent men of virtue rests on the view advanced earlier by Meno that virtue is managing the affairs of the city. That is to say that while the average Athenian would no doubt agree that virtue is something in the soul, if pushed to say what makes anyone a man of virtue he would likely respond by pointing to conduct of the sort that Meno listed.

This is not merely a question of what virtue is versus how you tell if someone has virtue. One way to frame the question is in terms of whether moral concepts, which are used to talk about persons (a good person or good character) as well as about conduct (a good deed), should be seen as primarily about one and only derivatively about the other. However, what depends on the answer is precisely how you teach virtue. If virtue is a matter of conduct, then it could perhaps be taught by constructing a list of rules and conditioning people to follow them. If, on the other hand, virtue is something in the soul, then if it is to be taught, what is called for is whatever would generate *therapeia*, or soul-tendence. (This is an issue that is directly addressed in *Republic*.)

Thus, the conflict represented by the two arguments arises out of conflicting views about the nature of virtue, and generation of the conflict is a way of focussing attention on the question of what virtue is.

While the views resulting in the conflict are associated with Meno and Anytus, the actual arguments in which they occur are made by Socrates as if they were his own. Thus, the art is manifested in this case by concentrating the views generating the conflict in the figure of Socrates. Plato makes Socrates embody the conflict that is an Athenian conflict and by articulating the views he does, Socrates exposes the unsettlement underlying the Athenian stance on this fundamental concept. The figure of Socrates is here just like the figure of Orestes in Aeschylus's *Oresteia*, in whom the conflict between the Homeric ideal and the emergent ideal of the democratic polis is embodied.

In *Oresteia*, the Homeric idea of justice as retribution rules throughout most of the trilogy. The spiral of vengeance afflicting the House of Atreus continues through Orestes, who is bound by the Homeric demands of justice to avenge the death of his father, Agamemnon, at the hands of his mother Clytemnestra. At the same time, he is bound by the same code to refrain from spilling kinship blood. The conflict within the code is thus captured in the figure of Orestes. Orestes takes refuge in the temple of Athena. There, the Assembly debates his fate and a tie vote is broken by the goddess herself in Orestes' favor. Thus, the Homeric idea of justice as retribution gives way to the idea of justice as determined through rational consideration of the good of the polis. The conflict is dramatically resolved in that way. The paradox represented by Orestes—that he ought to kill his mother and that he ought not to kill his mother—is resolved, not for Orestes, but for all after him by discarding the assumption about the nature of justice that led to the conflict in the first place.

In *Meno*, the conflict is left unresolved. Indeed, the terms of the conflict are not explicitly identified. It is left to the reader to identify the terms and recognize that resolution may be had through the same kind of transformation that takes place in *Oresteia*, the adoption of a new understanding of oneself.

Indirect Communication as Socratic Art

The Direct/Indirect Distinction

The idea of the Socratic art as operating by the concentration of the views of some portion of the culture in a single figure, who then articulates himself and thereby exposes the underlying conflict, is the idea operating in some of the pseudonymous works of Kierkegaard. It is one of the reasons that Kierkegaard referred to himself as a Socrates. He presented figures, who, by articulating themselves, exposed conflicts in the ways in which his culture thought about the most fundamental of matters, its understanding of what it is to be a person, its understanding of self. This tactic is part of the overall strategy that Kierkegaard called "indirect communication."

If we interpret the figure of Socrates in *Meno* as simply doing the kind of thing that we have come to take as the way of philosophy—asserting and arguing for positions[9]—we would have to see him as either holding conflicting views about whether or not virtue can be taught or, perhaps, as holding the view that virtue cannot be taught, since that is the last position for which he argues. Thus, reading *Meno* as made up by what has come to be standard philosophical fare, an example of "direct communication," would result in misinterpretation. Similarly, failing to take into account the fact of indirect communication in interpreting Kierkegaard's pseudonymous works will yield misinterpretation. This is particularly true with respect to the "paradoxical" elements of the works. It is those aspects of the works that I aim to address. Some account of what indirect communication is and the rationale for Kierkegaard's employment of it is in order first.

The distinction drawn by Kierkegaard between direct and indirect communication is well known and in addition to simply reviewing briefly Kierkegaard's representation of the distinction, I want to distinguish further between forms of communication that may fall within the broad category of what is not direct. Before

---

[9]This is, of course, not to assume that argumentation is simple and does not require analysis and interpretation.

embarking on that effort, I need to first set aside a view of Kierkegaard's use indirect communication as rooted in what has been
called "the problem of language."

Michael Strawser finds the seeds of indirect communication in
Kierkegaard's early realization "that there can be no solution to the
problem of language."[10] I present here Strawser's use of the text on
which he draws for his view.

> In a rich draft of *Johannes Climacus*, Kierkegaard concisely
> states what he more gradually develops in the text.
>
> > Immediately, then, everything is true; but can conscious-
> > ness not remain in this immediacy? If this immediacy and
> > that of animals were identical, then the question of con-
> > sciousness would be canceled; but the consequence of that
> > would be that a human being was an animal or that a human
> > being was inarticulate. That which therefore cancels immedi-
> > acy is language, if a person could not speak, he or she would
> > remain in immediacy.
> >
> > This, he thought, could be expressed thusly: immediacy
> > is reality, language is ideality, as I speak I produce the con-
> > tradiction. Thus, when I want to express sense perception,
> > the contradiction is there, for what I say is something rather
> > different than what I want to say. I cannot express reality in
> > language, since to characterize it I use ideality, which is a
> > contradiction, an untruth.
> >
> > The possibility of doubt, then lies in the duplicity of con-
> > sciousness (KW VII 255; JP III 2320; PIV B 14:6).
>
> Here Kierkegaard broaches the problem of language, and his
> analysis may be interpreted as providing grounds for the rejec-
> tion of a purely phenomenological language.[11]

Kierkegaard's conclusion "that there can be no solution to the
problem of language . . . provides," according to Strawser, "the
necessary philosophical background to understanding why Kierkegaard embarked on the sea of 'indirect communication'."

The first thing to note is that the passage presented by Strawser
does not include anything that is strictly speaking a "problem of
language." There is a problem for someone who would purport to
adequately represent an immediate perception by the use of lan-

---

[10]Michael Strawser, *Both/And: Reading Kierkegaard from Irony to Edification* (New
York: Fordham University Press, 1997) 77.

[11]Ibid., 75-76.

guage. To make this observation is not to nitpick, because it points to the second thing that needs to be noted. That is that the problem presented is inherent in engagement in a particular project. Johannes Climacus is concerned to see to what extent the Hegelian project can be carried out, and he captures the conflict that he sees as inherent in it. (This point should be borne in mind for an idea to be developed later in this chapter.) To see Climacus's realization here as foundational for Kierkegaard's view of his authorship is to presuppose that Kierkegaard is engaged in the same kind of project as Climacus. It is to see Kierkegaard as asking: What do I need to do to avoid the kind of conflict exposed in the project represented by Climacus? It is to see Kierkegaard as answering by saying that he needs to be more clever; he needs to be indirect.

The assumption that Kierkegaard is concerned about how to faithfully represent experience is at odds with what he says about indirect communication, however. "Scientific knowledge," Kierkegaard wrote, "can perhaps be beaten into a man, but one must beat the ethical out of him, as the corporal, precisely because he saw the soldier in the farmboy, may say: I will beat the soldier out of him . . . " (P VIII-2 81, 6). The imagery of beating something into someone and beating something out of someone suggests something of the distinction Kierkegaard makes. The obvious suggestion is that what is beaten into someone is something that the beating person has and the beaten person does not have. In the case of beating something out of someone, the suggestion is that the person being beaten already has the object.

On a more literal note, Kierkegaard wrote, "When I think of communication, I think of four things: (1) Object (2) Communicator (3) Receiver (4) Communication" (P VIII-2 B 83). (The fourth item that Kierkegaard here calls *communication* might be better referred to as the *vehicle of communication* to distinguish it from the entire phenomenon.) When the object is knowledge, the communication is direct. Now, in direct communication, the model is that of a transfer, in which one person directly transfers what one has to another person. In communication, the transfer is only symbolic. The one making the transference, the communicator, does not lose what is transferred. Rather, a sign is used to represent the object to the potential receiver. The ideal is for there to be a one-to-one relationship between the sign and the object—univocity. (This, of course, is not to say that there would be a one-to-one relationship between the constituent elements of the piece of knowledge and the elements of the sign, only that there would be some unique way of indicating that piece of knowledge.) While that condition is not met for signs in the overall linguistic system, it can be met within a particular piece of communication. Indeed, that is a condition for deductive inference. It can be achieved by the creation of technical language for the special disciplines.

When the object is not knowledge, but capability, communication is indirect, according to Kierkegaard. "All communication of knowledge is direct communication. All communication of capability is indirect communication" (P VIII-2 B 83). The distinction between knowing and doing is one that he saw as important for Christianity. "Christian dogmatics," he wrote, "I think, should be a development out of Christ's activity, insofar as Christ did not put forth any doctrine, but acted. He did not *teach that* there was deliverance for mankind, but he *delivered* mankind" (P I A 27; my emphases). In a similar vein, he wrote, "In relation to Socrates, it already holds true that the difficulty is not to understand his doctrine but to understand him. How much more is that the case with Christ" (P VIII-1 A 490). He also saw the distinction as personally important. "What I really lack is to be clear about what I am to do, not what I am to know except insofar as some understanding must precede every action" (P I A 75). Given the importance that Kierkegaard placed on the distinction, it is understandable that he would attribute importance to the distinction between communicating knowledge and communicating capability.

We need to consider, however, the claim that all communication of capability of knowledge is direct and all communication of capability is indirect. First of all, what does it mean? Is it a descriptive claim or is it a claim about what ought to be done? Can all communication be brought under the rubric of communication of knowledge or communication of capability? For communication that can be understood under one of those rubrics, is the disjunction exclusive?

Is the distinction between communication of knowledge and communication of capability a distinction between communication based on the intended upshot of the communication? That is, is the distinction between whether the communicator aims at affecting the cognitive state of the receiver as opposed to the conduct of the receiver? That way of understanding the distinction is certainly untenable. A simple case of giving directions to someone involves the imparting of information in a way that all parties would like to be unambiguous, but the ultimate upshot is that the receiver acts. Additionally, most teachers know that in order to enable students to understand some things, the student must be engaged in some activity. Role-playing can lead students to understand positions they might not otherwise come to comprehend. Thus, the attempt to understand the distinction between direct communication and indirect communication in terms of the intended upshot proves problematic.

Perhaps the distinction can be understood in terms of the ultimate upshot aimed at by the communicator. In the foregoing considerations, the intended upshot was complex, but its elements could perhaps be distinguished by their functioning as means to an ultimate end or as ultimate end. Clearly, in the case of direction-giving, the information is imparted in order to enable the receiver to act. In the case of role-playing in the classroom, the student is induced to act in order to be enabled to understand. Thus, we can identify the ultimate upshot aimed at in each case as either an action or a cognitive state. No one, however, would be inclined to think of direction-giving as a piece of indirect communication.

Perhaps direction-giving is a bad example. After all, the direction giver may not care one whit what the receiver does. His or her ultimate aim, it might be said, was simply the imparting of information. The same cannot be said, however, about imperatives, the issuance of a command or the making of a request, for example. We can imagine nonstandard cases such as a command in which a superior phrases a command as if it were a request ("Would you be so good as to bring the car around?") that might count as an "indirect command." Likewise, saying slyly in the presence of someone that one wished something were done, might be seen as indirectly requesting that it be done. Thus, the other person might respond by saying, "If you want me to X, why don't you just say so?" The usual case of imperatives, though, would hardly be construed as indirect communication. Therefore, indirect

communication cannot be understood in terms of the ultimate aim
of the communicator as inducement of the receiver to act.

Might it be that the difference between imperatives and indirect communication is not a difference in the ultimate aim of the
communicator, but in the initial capability of the receiver? After all,
the commander does not impart the ability to act to the person
commanded. That the person has the ability is the assumption
without which the command would be a farce. That would be like
commanding the blind to see. If indirect communication is the
communication of capability, as Kierkegaard says, perhaps the
communication consists in the imparting of the ability in some
way.

That hypothesis is at odds with the account of indirect communication given. The metaphor of beating something out of a man,
we recall, suggests that the receiver already has what is communicated. That is the view explicitly articulated by Kierkegaard. "The
ethical must be communicated as an art, because everyone knows
it. The corporal and the farmboy. The object of the communication
is therefore not knowledge but a realization" (P VIII-2 B, 81, 13).
It should be clear that "knowing it [the Ethical]" means "having
the capability of doing the Ethical." An even clearer indication of
that comes in the passage that says, "The Ethical presupposes that
everyone knows what the Ethical is. And why? Because the Ethical
demands that everyone shall realize the ethical in every moment,
and therefore one must know it" (P VIII-2 B 81,10). The communication of capability, then, is not to be seen as consisting in the
imparting of some ability that the receiver did not previously have.

If the receiver already has the capability, what is it that the
communicator communicates? An example Kierkegaard provides
is instructive. It is an example of a misunderstanding. Suppose,
Kierkegaard suggests, that an officer tells a recruit to stand erect,
and the recruit replies that he will. Suppose, further, that the
officer then tells the recruit that he is not to talk during drill, and
the recruit replies that he will not; you just have to tell me that.
"Officer: 'For Satan, you are not to talk during drill.' Recruit: 'Yes,
yes, don't be angry; if I know it, I will not talk during drill' " (P
VIII-2 B 81, 14). What is the misunderstanding here? It is the
recruit's interpretation of the order as something he is to take as
true on the authority of the officer. It is his failure to recognize that

the appropriate response is behaving a certain way, not recognition of the truth of something.

If the example above shows something of what Kierkegaard had in mind, it also serves to falsify the descriptive statement that all communication of capability is indirect—if communication of capability is inducement to act. The failure of communication did not stem from the fact that it was direct, but from the recruit's misunderstanding. The communication, direct as it is, would be successful in most cases. Similarly, athletes may have to be told directly where and how to position themselves and what moves to make in certain situations. That is a part of communicating the capability of playing the game. Coaches also do things sometimes to inspire players to perform at their highest level. Posting disparaging remarks made by the opposition, for example, is a way of motivating players to perform in ways that they might not otherwise have performed. The aim is to elicit the realization of an ability, not to instill an ability that was not there before. In the case of the officer and the recruit, what the officer wants is not simply the obedience of this or that order, but the adoption of an orientation—thinking of oneself as a soldier—from which certain unspecified behaviors will follow. Similarly, the coach does not want performance of this or that athletic feat, but adoption of the stance of the committed athlete. The imparting of information may be a part of the overall project of inducing that commitment.

I have been led away from talking about communication of capability as aiming at inducement of action to talking about it as inducement to adopting some sense of oneself, from which some unspecified conduct would flow. Is the distinction between direct and indirect communication, then, simply the distinction between imparting information and inspiring behavior? Is the coach in the example engaged in indirect communication as Kierkegaard understands it? The example of the coaching tactic is surely a case of communication that is not direct in the sense that there is no knowledge that is the object of communication. The coach need not even tell the players what the coach wants done, although what the coach wants done is by no means a mystery. Indeed, the coach may refer to the posting in a pregame meeting, and, with evangelical verve, exhort his/her charges to show their pride and prove the opinion of the opposition to be on the far side of lunacy. Here, what the communicator aims at is action that is relatively specif-ic—good performance in this game today. Might that be different from Kierkegaardian indirect communication insofar as the latter is concerned with action over a period of time. After all, the de-mand of the Ethical is that it be realized at every moment, not just in this or that situation.

Why might it be thought desirable to distinguish Kierke-gaardian indirect communication from phenomena such as the devices of a coach? If the aim is to avoid linking indirect communi-cation with undesirable companions such as propaganda and advertising, the strategy will not work. Propagandistic devices may aim at something specific such as the desecration of some object or they may aim at inculcating an attitude that will influence behavior towards some group over a person's lifetime. Similarly, advertising may usher in a particular purchase or it might generate self-images that result in certain choices over a long term. So, we cannot find the distinction that avoids an unhappy alliance in the specific performance/general conduct difference.

The Pragmatic Rationale

We may find out more about Kierkegaard's view and, conse-quently, whether or not there is basis for distinguishing Kierke-gaardian indirect communication from other nondirect strategies if we inquire into the reasons Kierkegaard thought it important to be mindful of the distinction between direct and indirect communi-cation. There are two kinds of reasons Kierkegaard had for indirect communication. One is pragmatic; the other is ethical, in the broad sense. These two reasons, it will be seen, reinforce each other.

The pragmatic consideration for indirect communication is explicitly addressed by Plato. The passage in *Sophist* previously referred to considers alternative ways of educating. While it speaks only about the elenchus, the point is applicable to the wider range of strategies we saw in *Meno*.

> But we have still to consider whether education admits of any further division deserving a name. . . .
> There is the time-honored mode which our fathers commonly practiced toward their sons, which is still adopted by many—either of roughly reproving their errors, or of gently

advising them—which varieties may be correctly included under the general term of admonition. . . .

But whereas some appear to have arrived at the conclusion that all ignorance is involuntary, and that no one who thinks himself wise is willing to learn any of those things in which he is conscious of his own cleverness, and that the admonitory sort of education gives much trouble and does little good. . . . Accordingly, they set to work to eradicate the spirit of conceit in another way. (*Sophist* 229d-230b)

The rationale for the unorthodox method is clear. Orthodoxy does not work well, and there is an explanation for the ineffectiveness of the orthodox approach. If you think you know, you have no motivation to inquire. We saw that in our examination of *Meno*.

There is no question here as to whether or not the educator can say directly what one wants the pupil to learn. (Clearly Socrates could have said: "Meno, your arrogance is standing in the way of your making any genuine inquiry into virtue. You think you already know what it is, and what you are doing is inviting my participation in the game of displaying uncommon wisdom. Instead of our playing that game, let us look into the matter seriously.") Poul Lübcke makes this point about Kierkegaard's use of indirect communication. Can the message in ethical and religious indirect communication be directly stated? "Of course we *could* do it, but it is not what we *ought* to do. Instead we ought to take the object and the message about it as given and pass from the semantic to the pragmatic level of speech, so as to concentrate on the pragmatic task of motivating the listener to do what he knows to be his duty."[12] Lübcke does not make clear whether the "ought" he uses here is a pragmatic or ethical "ought."[13] It is apparently a pragmatic "ought," since, as Lübcke explains, the object in ethical communication is taken to be known by all, and it would be "pointless to spell it out."[14] Additionally, Lübcke points out that the perlocutionary effect aimed at by Kierkegaard's strategy is

---

[12]Poul Lübcke, "Kierkegaard and Indirect Communication," *History of European Ideas* 12/1 (1990): 34.

[13]The pragmatic/ethical distinction I make here should not be confused with the distinction in the passage by Lübcke between the pragmatic and semantic dimensions of language.

[14]Lübcke, "Kierkegaard and Indirect Communication," 34.

"confirmation of the religious way of life," and since "confirmation is a kind of decision, Kierkegaard thought he had to use . . . indirect [communication]. . . . [O]ne person *can* never force another man to decide."[15] The suggestion here is that of a means/ends consideration that is essentially pragmatic—about what *can* be effective. This pragmatic rationale for indirect communication seems to be present in Kierkegaard's remark quoted earlier that ethical must be beaten out of a man. There, we will recall, the contrast was between what can be done (beating knowledge into someone) and what must be done (beating capability out of someone).[16]

The judgment in favor of the pragmatic propriety of indirect communication depends on some assumptions about the intended audience. The impediment to making a decision may not be of the sort that would call for indirection. A bewildered person may seek counsel about what to do when it is not clear what the options are or what the ramifications of the options are. Someone, in all naivete, simply may not have thought of the significance of courses of action one habitually follows. In those kinds of cases, direct communication may well do the job of inducing someone to decide and may well be appropriate. ("Wow! I hadn't thought of that!" may well be the response to a direct communication.) If it is the case, however, that the fact of not having thought of the significance of habit is accompanied by pride in one's position or the conviction of the rightness of one's course, direct communication would likely fall on deaf ears. That was the case with Meno, and hence it was the kind of situation that was ripe for a Socrates.

That was indeed the situation in nineteenth century Denmark, in Kierkegaard's judgment. On a number of scores, Kierkegaard thought that his contemporaries mistakenly thought of themselves as Christian and needed to be prodded into seeing the need to decide to become a Christian. The most prominent point is, of course, the union of Christian theology and Hegelian philosophy, particularly as espoused by H. L. Martensen. There was, also, the

---

[15]Ibid., 36; emphasis mine.

[16]This is not to ignore the fact that the Danish word for 'must' (*må*) is, like the English, ambiguous. It could be the 'must' of practical necessity or the 'must' of obligation. The example of the recruit makes it clear, however, that the 'must' of practical necessity is meant.

union of Church and State, championed by Bishop Mynster in the late 1840s, which effectively expressed the assumption that the role of the citizen and the role of a Christian were completely compatible, perhaps even identical.[17] There was the Romantic element descended from Oehlenschläger, for whom religiosity was a union with nature that was captured in the poetic point of view. Bishop Mynster was at times in alliance with proponents of this version of Christianity. The different misunderstandings of Christianity within an officially Christian society would be the appropriate targets for Socratic attention. Just as the question for Socrates was how to introduce Meno to virtue when Meno was convinced that he knew what virtue was and that he had it, the question for Kierkegaard was how to introduce Christianity to his contemporaries when they thought of themselves as Christians.

The Ethical Rationale

The considerations Kierkegaard made were not only pragmatic, however. Kierkegaard thought of himself as Socrates and, like Climacus of *Fragments*, he thought that Socrates expressed the (ethically) highest possible relationship between one person and another. That highest relationship is one of equality, since with respect to the object of communication, everyone is assumed to be essentially in the same position. Nonetheless, Kierkegaard understood that there was sometimes a tension between maintaining that relationship, on the one hand, and the desire to do good as well as the ethical requirement of doing good, on the other hand (the classic tension between the demands of equality and the demands of benevolence). He wrote, "I wonder if Socrates was so cold, I wonder if it did not pain him that Alcibiades could not understand him" (P V B 43). That remark captures Kierkegaard's desire to be more forthcoming than indirection permitted. That there was a question of ethical permissibility of undertaking to influence someone's decision is captured in the following.

Do I have the right (however much I would like to have someone share my view) to use my art to win over someone; is

---

[17]See Bruce Kirmmse, *Kierkegaard in Golden Age Denmark* (Bloomington and Indianapolis: Indiana University Press, 1990) 132-35.

it not to deceive him in some fashion. When he sees me moved, enthusiastically stirred, etc., so he adopts my view, consequently for an entirely different reason than I and and untrue reason.

Most people probably do not understand at all what the talk is about that one who has an art to use shall use it; indeed he who does not use it is an immoral person who does not recognize duty, is without seriousness, is selfish, etc. Answer: Bah! (P V A 47)

About his entire career as of 1847, he wrote:

One can now do with me what one will, insult me, envy me, stop reading me, beat me, kill: that which one cannot in all eternity deny, which was my idea and my life, that it was one of the most original thoughts in a long time and the most original in the Danish language: that Christendom needed a midwife [Majeutiker] and I understood being that—while no one understood appreciating it. (P VIII 1A 42)

The need for a midwife, a practitioner of indirect communication, is not, then, just the result of pragmatic considerations, but of ethical ones.

How, though, should we understand the ethical consideration? Is there is a fundamental distinction between Kierkegaard's indirect communication and the forms of nondirect communication discussed before? The use of rhetorical devices that aim at specific acts or at an orientation towards specific kinds of acts may involve treating the receiver of the communication as means only. It may aim at shaping the world in a way chosen by the communicator.[18] If the communicator is successful, the receiver acts without first reflecting. Kierkegaardian indirect communication, or rather, indirect communication as used by Kierkegaard, aims at shaping the world in such a way that each recipient of the communication is fundamentally free to choose to shape the world as one sees fit. In fact, if the effort is successful, the receiver comes to see that one

---

[18]I say here that these strategies may involve treating the receiver as object only instead of saying that they do, because the receiver may be in his/her position voluntarily with the understanding that the communicator is to do the sorts of things one does as part of a cooperative enterprise. That, I take it, is the situation with many athletic teams.

must choose; one is induced to reflect. With specific reference to *Either/Or*, Kierkegaard wrote:

> The reader stepped into a self-acting relationship to the book, which is what I wanted, what I had strived to contribute to by complete abstention from any remark on design in the work, and besides I could not know better than any other reader if it was that way. The design was a task of self-action and to press my interpretation on the reader seemed to me an impudent and insulting interference. (P IV B 59)

About himself, he wrote:

> My destiny seems to be that I shall recite the truth as far as I can discover it—in this way—that it occurs with the simultaneous annihilation of all possible authority. While I remain without authority, in the highest degree unreliable in the eyes of men, I tell the truth and thereby bring them into the contradiction from which they can only be helped by themselves appropriating the truth. . . . (P IV A 87)

The foregoing gives us an understanding of how indirect communication can be used in a morally repugnant way and how it may be used in a morally permissible way. When it is used in a way that treats the receiver as means only, it is morally unacceptable. When it is used in a way that respects the autonomy of the receiver, it is morally acceptable.

That is not the distinction we ultimately aimed at understanding, however. We aimed at understanding the distinction between direct communication and indirect communication such that the former is seen as morally unacceptable in some circumstances. The first step would be, of course, to get clear about just what the distinction is between direct communication and indirect communication. We have seen that Kierkegaard certainly overstated the case in saying that all communication of capability is indirect. That claim is neither descriptively nor prescriptively correct. Kierkegaard understood himself to be engaged in communication of "the Ethical" or "the Ethical-Religious." It may be that what he says about communication of capability is only meant to apply to that. We need to see if understanding the claim as so restricted makes a difference.

Communicating the Ethical

Kierkegaard understands "the Ethical" as constitutive of what it is to be a person. "The Ethical" is the notion of the essential-human. Although in *Either/Or* and *Fear and Trembling*, a Kant-ian/Hegelian understanding of "ethical" operates, the use of the term "the Ethical" is independent of any particular ethical theory. That is to say, whether one is an Aristotelian, utilitarian, Kantian, one understands what is required by the ethical as binding on one insofar as one is a person. Those ethical theories do not differ in that respect. Rather, they differ in terms of just what is understood as constituting the Ethical and, consequently, on how one goes about determining what is required in any particular circumstance. This notion of the universal bindingness of the Ethical is what makes it to be the idea of the essential-human.

> Real communication or teaching in relation to the Ethical and the Ethical-Religious is upbringing [*Opdragelse*] With upbringing one becomes what one is essentially regarded as being. . . . Upbring-ing begins by regarding the one who is to be brought up as *kata dynamin* [potentially] being what he will become and by seeing him in that way, brings it out of him. He draws [*drager*] it up [*op*]. . . . (P VIII-2 B 82, 12)

When "the Ethical" is understood as the essential-human, it becomes clear why Kierkegaard would see an essential difference between communicating knowledge and communicating "the Ethical." In communication of knowledge, there is an essential difference between the communicator and the receiver with respect to the object of communication. The communicator has the object, and the receiver does not. Direct communication reflects this essential difference, insofar as the communicator, on his/her own authority, undertakes to change the relationship between the receiver and the object. (Providing reasons is a way of trying to show that the authority is grounded and to bring the receiver into the same relationship with the object that the communicator enjoys.) In communication of "the Ethical," there is no essential difference between the communicator and the receiver, according to Kierkegaard. Everyone has "the object" and in the same degree. That being the case, for someone to undertake to communicate "the Ethical" directly would be for that someone to adopt the stance of essential superiority. Thus, it is respect for the principle of equality that requires indirect communication of "the Ethical."

> With respect to the ethical one man cannot have authority in relation to another, because God is the master teacher and every man a learner. If one man would say to another: Do the ethical, it is as if in the same moment one heard God say to that important man: Nonsense, my friend, it is you who should do it. (P VIII-2 B 81, 16)

The divine rebuke in the hypothetical above makes clear that the direct communication of the ethical is something that is understood as prohibited, not something that is understood as an impossibility. What is also indicated is that the prohibition is due to a mistaking of one's place in relation to another ("that important man"); direct communication, the passage says, denies the essential equality of persons with respect to what is communicated.

Why would it be thought that there is that difference?[19] After all, in the communication of knowledge what happens is that the receiver realizes a capacity that one already had, the capacity to acquire knowledge or understanding. The difference is that, typically, there is not a doubt about whether or not the receiver has the capacity. When there is some doubt, that is when some strategy other than the straightforward presentation of the facts ("Facts" is here a stand-in for ordinary factual information, as well as theoretical and conceptual claims.) is appropriate. That is when a teacher may, for example, engage students in some exercises or present some analogies that incline the students to realize that they can comprehend the matter at hand. The teacher assumes that the capacity is there, but that some work needs to be done to enable the student to realize the capacity. Equality with respect to having the capacity is assumed. That assumption is not always well-founded, however, since there is a difference in intellectual capacity among people. Once the student gets to the point of seeing that one can come to know or understand, other tools that might be considered straightforward may be employed, direct communication, if you will. There is no assumption of equality with respect to the specific content of the direct communication.

---

[19] I thank Steve Lee for nudging me in the direction of thinking about this.

Thus, in matters of knowledge, there is no equality with respect to capacity, and there is no assumed equality with respect to the specific content of a communication. That inequality, however, is not inequality with respect to personhood.

Suppose someone says, "The Ethical requires that you love your neighbor." That would be direct communication. There is the straightforward representation of a relationship between two ideas—the idea of the Ethical and the idea of the requirement of loving your neighbor. The communication is similar to (not just like) saying, "A square has four sides." Typically, it only makes sense to make either of those two statements if you think that the reader or hearer may not know the truth you are presenting. You *invite* the audience to interpret your statement as one that is to be understood as true in the sense that it articulates a thought that is adequate to the thing.[20]

Now, suppose someone says, "You should love your neighbor." Recalling the passage with the imagined divine rebuke, we would say that this is also a case of direct communication. Unlike the case mentioned above, this would not be a factual claim, but an imperative. It is like the case in which the recruit is told not to talk. The recruit's problem is that he understood the command as the reporting of a rule: there is a rule that says that you should not talk during drill. The imperative here may also be (mis)understood as the reporting of a rule: There is a rule that says that you should love your neighbor. The form of the presentation permits interpretation as the reporting of a rule, which report may be true or false.

Is that, perhaps, the distinction between direct and indirect communication? Is it that the former either *invites* (as in the first case) or *permits* (as in the second case) interpretation as a factual presentation? Let us imagine someone who constructs an elegant and elaborate story to incline the reader in the direction of loving his/her neighbor. I can well imagine that person's being asked by an interviewer, "So, what are you trying to tell us?" Nor is sophistication in strategy any protection. If someone went so far as to try to defy interpretation as factual presentation by giving the

---

[20]The "thing" being talked about here happens to be a thought or idea, the idea of the Ethical. The statement purports to be an elaboration of that idea.

communication a paradoxical character, he could still be sure that he would be read as saying that he wants to say that the subject matter is elusive, ineffable, or something of that sort, such that the truth is not capable of being captured by ordinary locutions. So it looks as if the difference between direct and indirect communication is not to be found in whether or not the form is such as to invite or permit interpretation as factual presentation.

Might the difference consist in whether or not the form is such as to *discourage* interpretation as factual presentation? How would that be different from the former cases? While the discourse might permit interpretation as factual presentation, it would contain features that would discourage that kind of interpretation. The author would be unable to guarantee the manner of reception of the work, but there would be signs that point to interpretation as calling for action rather than an essentially cognitive response. Why should we expect the form to carry the burden of discouraging misinterpretation? The form of what we identify as a piece of indirect communication may be identical to a piece of direct communication. "When the child must be weaned, the mother blackens her breast" may be a piece of indirect communication (an invitation to consider one's relationship to a dependent person) or it may be a report of child-rearing practice. In one context, interpretation as factual presentation would be ludicrous; in another context, it would not. So it could not be the form that makes the difference.[21]

The Art in Communication

Perhaps the effort to uncover some singular principle for distinguishing direct communication from indirect communication is misguided. After all, we are considering the difference between something that can be understood as art from something that is not art. Art is distinguished from science. It is also distinguishable from politics, religion, mathematics, etc. What might be said in the one case may be different from what one says in other cases. It might be better to consider the way in which we distinguish

---

[21]I am aware that it is the entire work from which the line here is taken that constitutes the effort in indirect communication. Nonetheless, the line by itself may well function as a piece of indirect communication.

between something that falls under a particular genre of art from something that does not. If indirect communication is a form of art using words, we might try to distinguish it from, say, an essay in history or a sermon. (This is not to rule out the possibility of indirect communication that uses a medium other than words. It is not immediately clear what would count as direct communication in other media; thus, it is not clear what indirect communication without that contrast would be.)

Consider, for example, Sophocles' *Oedipus Rex*. It is certainly a dramatic work, a tragedy. Critics generally see it as, at least, saying something about the peril of our ignoring the hidden powers of the universe and relying on our own wits. The same kind of point might be made in a sermon or a lecture, and we would not be inclined to regard the sermon or lecture as a work of art. What is the difference? One might be inclined to say that insofar as *Oedipus Rex* makes the point, it does so indirectly, while the sermon or the lecture does so directly. How is that? Is it that the former leaves it to the audience to figure out what the point is while the latter does not? If so, how does it leave it to the audience? What does it do that constitutes leaving it to the audience and, consequently, qualifies it as indirect? The dramatic work presents a possible world in which the audience might locate itself and which is such that the audience may feel more or less empathy towards some figures presented. Characters may articulate their feelings towards each other, themselves, and their circumstances, but there is typically no authoritative editorial voice that calls for a specific response. That is the sense in which it is left to the members of the audience to decide whether or not what happens with the figures is something that connects with their lives in such a way as to evoke sympathy, antipathy, self-reflection, or action. There is no voice that is identifiably the author's that says, "If you ignore the gods and rely solely on the power of reason, you will suffer."

Clearly, a dramatic work may move in the direction of being didactic, that is, of being relatively explicit about a point to be taken. To the extent that it does that, the work is criticized negatively as a work of art. To call a work that is presented as art didactic is to pan it. On the other hand, a lecture may move in the direction of being artistic performances. A lecturer may adopt the stance of a character in order to add dramatic punch, if you will, to the presentation. The right balance would have to be struck to avoid missing the objective and, thereby, failing as a lecture. The point here is different from the recognition that a work of art may incorporate direct discourse without changing its character as a work of art. (John Updike's *Roger's Version* does not become a philosophical treatise because a character argues against a natural explanation of the origination of life on earth.)

What is involved is expressed in Johannes Climacus's remarks about the subjective thinker.

> But existence-actuality cannot be communicated, and the subjective thinker has his own actuality in his own ethical existence. If actuality is to be understood by a third party, it must be understood as possibility, and a communicator who is conscious of this will therefore see to it, precisely in order to be oriented to existence, that his existence-communication is in the form of possibility. (CUP 358)

Climacus's concern is that ethical requirement not be communicated in such a way as to invite admiration rather than appropriation. My concern at this point is not with the rationale given but with the understanding of what the communication is like. If something is presented as an actuality, it can, of course, be received as a possibility for the audience. The presentation of the actuality of Michael Jordan can inspire genuine resolve to "be like Mike." That requires essential identification with Jordan as opposed to viewing him as exceptional. (The fact that Jordan is exceptional and not representative is the sad part, unless one understands what is to be emulated as realizing one's potential, rather than achieving NBA stardom.) So, the presentation of possibility involves the creation of figures with whom the audience can identify, figures who display possibilities, then, that the audience can see as its own.

That is the work of the poet as Aristotle understood it.

> [T]he poet's function is to describe, not the thing that has happened, but a kind of thing that might happen, that is, what is possible as being probable or necessary. The distinction between historian and poet is not in the one writing prose and the other verse—you might put the work of Herodotus into verse, and it would still be a species of history; it consists really in this, that the one describes the thing that has been, and the other a kind of thing that might be. Hence poetry is something more philosophic

and of graver import than history, since its statements are of the nature rather of universals, whereas those of history are singular. (Poetics 1451a36-1451b8)

That sort of poetic production is what Kierkegaard was engaged in, as has been so eloquently argued by Louis Mackey in *Kierkegaard: A Kind of Poet*.[22]

If Herodotus's work were put into verse, how would we know that it is a species of history? Aristotle's view is that the nature of the subject matter is what determines the genre. If the work is about actuality, it is history; if it is about possibility, it is poetry. (Not just any possibility, mind you, but what is universal.) Is there some mark by which one distinguishes the possible from the actual, though, in a written work? One way to make that distinction is for the author to undermine himself/herself as authority for what is said in the work. That is done in a novel by having the author simply not appear as a figure or commentator in the work. So, even though the author's name usually appears on the cover, we do not typically ascribe to the author the views, feelings, or experiences that are given in the work.[23] Kierkegaard's pseudonymity takes his removal as authoritative voice a step further. Conversely, if a story appears in a newspaper, because the publisher offers it up under his/her banner, it is regarded as factual claims. That same story offered up in a flyer and not attributed to anyone would be regarded differently. Thus, it does not seem that there is something about the form of the sentences or the form of the entire structure that makes the work a presentation of possibility, that makes it a work of art, but rather the relationship between the work and its maker. Something about the form of the sentences and the form of the entire structure may have much to do with how good a work of art it is, but it seems

---

[22]Louis Mackey, *Kierkegaard: A Kind of Poet* (Philadelphia: University of Pennsylvania Press, 1971).

[23]The point here is one that is apparently acknowledged by Gore Vidal in a letter to Louis Auchicloss: "I'm always interested when you're telling a story or when you're writing an essay; my only quibble with you is when you let your characters get into discussions and do your essay telling for you" (*The New Yorker*, 9 June 1997, 76).

that Aristotle is right that the form does not determine the nature of the piece.

If we revisit Climacus's remarks about communication of existential reality, we see that it is precisely the distinction between presenting something as having actually happened and something that is possible that is important to the subjective thinker.

> Instead of presenting the good in the form of actuality, as is ordinarily done, that this and that person have actually lived and have actually done this and thus transforming the reader into an observer, an admirer, an appraiser,it should be presented in the form of possibility. Then whether or not the reader wants to exist in it is placed as close as possible to him. Possibility operates with the ideal human being (not with regard to difference but with regard to the universal), who is related to every human being as requirement. (CUP 358-359)

The only distinction that is clear from this is the distinction between whether or not the presenter is vouching for the validity (factual truth or ethical weight) of what is said. Note that this is not about whether the sentences in question constitute factual claims, but whether the author presents them as claims for which the author vouches.

Given the nature of the pseudonymous works as efforts in indirect communication and the understanding of indirect communication as involving the absence of authority on the part of the communicator, it would be a mistake to take what is said in the works as the exposition of Kierkegaard's views. The older debate about whether the Absolute Paradox in *Fragments* and *Postscript* should be understood as above the reason or against the reason has given way to a debate as to whether or not Kierkegaard espouses a volitionalist epistemology and the tenability of his epistemology, whatever it is.[24] The terms in which those debates are cast assume that Kierkegaard is engaged in the kind of enterprise in which philosophers have been traditionally understood as engaged. That ignores the fact of indirect communication. When that fact is not

---

[24]On the former debate, see Benjamin Daise, "Kierkegaard and the Absolute Paradox," *Journal of the History of Philosophy* 14/1 (January 1976): 63-68. On the latter, see Benjamin Daise, "The Will to Truth in Kierkegaard's Philosophical Fragments," *Philosophy of Religion* 31 (January 1992): 1-12.

ignored, we are able to see that the articulation of the puzzling idea referred to as the Absolute Paradox emerges from a strategy that is driven by a particular kind of conflict. Understanding the concepts and claims made in the text in which that conflict occurs requires attention to what is done to develop the conflict. When that is done, the irrelevance of epistemological and metaphysical disputes becomes apparent. To engage in that debate would be like engaging in the debate about moral relativism. It is an evasion, in Kierkegaard's view.

> Suppose someone says: I must first know what the Ethical is. How specious, especially since we are used to that reasoning from childhood. But the Ethical responds quite consistently: Scoundrel, will you quibble and seek to evade? He says: There are indeed different conceptions of the Ethical in different lands and different times. How does one bring that doubt to a close? From a scholarly point of view, the matter grows to volumes and does not stop, but the Ethical holds on to the doubter and says that is not your concern; You shall do the Ethical in every moment and are ethically liable for every moment you squander. (P VIII-2 B 81, 10)

Kierkegaard's understanding of his enterprise as indirect communication is reaffirmed in his explicit thoughts about communication. He writes:

> The difference between upbringing in relation to the Ethical and the Ethical-Religious is simply that the Ethical is as a matter of course the universal human, but religious (Christian) upbringing must first communicate knowledge. Ethically a person is as such knowledgeable about the Ethical, but Christianly speaking one is not as such knowledgeable about the religious; here there must first be a little communication—but then the same relationship as in the Ethical begins again. The teaching, the communication must not be as knowledge, but upbringing, training, art teaching. Herein lies my service with the pseudonyms: within Christianity to have discovered the maieutic. (P VIII-2 B 82, 13)

When an author takes that kind of position, we should avoid attributing to him words that are put into the mouths of his pseudonyms. Indeed, as we shall see, we need to be careful even about attributing to the pseudonym views that are articulated by his words.

Chapter 2

The Question of *Philosophical Fragments*

There are three questions on the title page of *Philosophical Fragments*: "Can a historical point of departure be given for an eternal consciousness; how can such a point of departure be of more than historical interest; can an eternal happiness be built on historical knowledge?" The first chapter opens with this question: "Can the truth be taught?"[1] (PF 9; SV 6, 15). On the page before the one with the opening question, there is a statement referred to as *Propositio* or hypothesis. It reads: "The question is asked by some unknowing person, who does not even know what gave rise to his questioning in this way" (PF 9; SV 6, 13). About what question is this being said? For what reason? The use of the definite article indicates that the statement is not about the asking of questions in general, and the placement of the statement points to the four mentioned as the obvious candidates. We will consider the question opening chapter 1 first.

We have seen that the question posed by Meno in the opening of the dialogue bearing his name was not generated by any genuine concern that he had about how virtue is acquired. Indeed, Meno was shown to be ignorant of what virtue is. His defensive responses to Socrates' criticisms showed that he was not aware of the conceit behind his asking. So, it can surely be said that the "Socratic question" in that case was asked in the manner stated in *Propositio*. That gives us reason to see the question opening chapter 1 as the object of *Propositio*. That is so, because the manner in which Johannes Climacus, the pseudonymous author of *Fragments*, goes about arriving at an answer to the question he poses points to conceit behind his asking. In fact, Kierkegaard wrote about *Fragments*, "To act as if Christianity were the invention of Johannes

---

[1]The Danish word *Læres* can be translated as "learned" or "taught." Since the Socratic question is "Can virtue be taught?" it is preferable to translate *Læres* as taught.

Climacus is precisely the biting satire on philosophy's impudence towards it" (P VI A 84). This pretense is undertaken in chapter 1 under the guise of a "Thought-Project." Climacus acknowledges that in the final chapter:

> As is well known, Christianity is the only historical phenomenon that, the historical notwithstanding—indeed, precisely by means of the historical—has wanted to be the single individual's point of departure for his eternal consciousness, has wanted to interest him otherwise than merely historically, has wanted to base his happiness on his relation to something purely historical. No philosophy (for it is only for thought), no mythology (for it is only for the imagination), no historical knowledge (which is for memory) has ever had this idea— of which in this connection one can say with all multiple meanings that it did not arise in any human heart. To a certain extent, however, I have wanted to forget this, and, employing the unrestricted method of a hypothesis, I have assumed that the whole thing was a whimsical idea of my own, one that I did not wish to abandon before I had thought it through. (PF 109; SV 6,98)

Thus it is clear from remarks in the papers and in the text itself that the views arrived at in the text were not arrived at in the way that the text initially purports to arrive at them. We also see that the ostensible method adopted in chapter 1 in response to the opening question was seen as responsive to the questions of the title page. When we compare Climacus's acknowledgement with Kierkegaard's draft of the "Thought-Project," we see that Climacus's supposed method allows him to assume the position that Kierkegaard sees as ascribable to the age. In the draft, instead of having Climacus say simply that he, methodologically, wanted to forget that it was only Christianity that proposed to provide a historical point of departure for an eternal consciousness, what is said is that "However, we will forget this, and have forgotten it, as if Christianity never existed . . . " (P V B 3, 2). The methodology mimics forgetting.

The Ostensible Method

The method proposed by Climacus involves four steps: (1) articulating the answer to the question from the Socratic perspective, (2) eliciting the implications of that view, (3) negating the

Socratic perspective by assuming the denial of one of its implications, and (4) eliciting the implications of the assumption constituted by the negation of the Socratic perspective. This mimics the procedure known as the Eleatic method that was used by Parmenides, of Elea, in his "The Way of Truth." In that work, Parmenides is trying to establish what can be said truthfully about reality, what can be known about what there is.[2] The alternatives he considers are: "It is (thus)." and "It is not (thus)." There is an assertion and its negation. The latter, Parmenides says, is utterly false and the former is the way of truth. (A third option, the conjunction of the other two, is called the way of seeming.) He extracts what he sees as the implications of the true way in order to construct his ontology. Since the assertion of change involves saying that what is at one time at another time is not, the assertion of change is false. Since coming into being and perishing involve change, these do not occur. Since plurality involves the assertion that what is differs from what is, that is, is not what is, that assertion is false. So, what is has the following attributes: changelessness, eternity, singularity.

Like Parmenides, Climacus considers two possible responses to his question. The first is given from the Socratic perspective as it is derived from the story of Recollection. Every person already has the truth. (This is the first step.) Consequently (second step), no person can be of more than occasional significance to another. That is, no one can impart the truth to anyone else; one could, at most, provide the occasion for another's discovery for himself that he has the truth. The moment of discovery, then, is of no essential significance. It is only accidental, since the essential condition for discovery was already there (PF 9-13).

The third and fourth steps consist in formulating the radically un-Socratic hypothesis by denying one of the consequences elicited above and extracting the implications of that denial. "If the situation is to be different, then the moment in time must have . . . decisive significance. . . . With this presupposition, let us now examine the relations involved in the question: Can the truth be [taught]?" (PF 13; SV 6, 15). Adopting this presupposition, Clima-

---

[2]See Charles Kahn, "The Thesis of Parmenides," *Review of Metaphysics* 22:704-706.

cus's hypothesis, Climacus, by *modus tollens*, negates the Socratic view. From that negation, he elicits the following implications:

1. [T]he seeker up until that moment [of acquisition of the truth] must not have possessed the truth . . . (PF 13).
2. [T]he teacher must bring it [the truth] to him . . . and [a]long with it, he must provide him with the condition for understanding the truth . . . (PF 14).
3. [This] must be done by the god himself (PF 15).
4. [The seeker must have been deprived of the truth and this deprivation] cannot have been due to an act of the god . . . (PF 15).
5. [I]t must therefore have been due to himself (PF 15).
6. [To be freed from the bondage of untruth] . . . first of all, he must will it (PF 16).
7. He will not be able to set himself free (PF 17).
8. [A] teacher who gives him the condition again and along with it the truth . . . [is to be called] a savior . . . (PF 17).
9. [A]s a result of receiving the condition in the moment, his course took the opposite direction, or he was turned around. Let us call this change conversion . . . (PF 18).
10. [T]his conversion cannot take place without its being assimilated into his consciousness or without his becoming aware that it was through his own fault [that he had been in untruth]. . . . [The sorrow] over having been so long in the former state . . . is repentance (PF 19).

Noting the content of those ten points and the language used in them, we would not need to await Climacus's acknowledgement in chapter 5 that he was presenting Christianity as the radically un-Socratic alternative. He appears to have derived these tenets of Christianity from a simple hypothesis. Since Climacus's response to the question is only a feigned invention to a question apparently asked out of idle curiosity, we should see the origin of the question (like the origin of the response) as different from what Climacus supposedly takes it to be. In other words, since Climacus is presented as asking simply out of curiosity, he is presented as asking in ignorance of what actually gave rise to the question. He is, thus, likened to Meno, and the opening of chapter 1, featuring a question without any vital context, parallels exactly what happens in *Meno*.

If it is the case, as I claim, that the questions of the title page raise essentially the same issue as the question opening chapter 1, then the problem of identifying the referent of *Propositio* would be solved or, perhaps more accurately, dissolved. It is necessary, however, to understand exactly what issue is raised.

The Opening Question

The opening question—"Can the truth be taught?"—is said by Climacus to be "a Socratic question or became that by way of the Socratic question whether virtue can be taught—for virtue was again defined as insight" (PF 9). How should we understand that?[3] Let us first understand the Socratic question. What is it about? The term that is generally translated as "virtue" is *arete*, which might well be translated as "excellence." It refers to that condition that makes a thing to be essentially the kind of thing that it is. Thus, it refers to the ideal to which a thing must conform in order to realize its essential self, to behave as a thing of its kind ought to behave. That is what is behind these questions by Socrates in *Republic*: "Does each thing to which a particular task is assigned also have its virtue. . . . Could the eyes perform their function well if they did not possess their own virtue . . . ?" (*Republic* 353b). "Each thing" includes human beings, and exactly what constitutes virtue for human beings is hardly a settled matter among the ancients. Among the Homeric Greeks, it is the warrior/hero who exhibits *arete* and representing a later age, Meno ticks off a list of different *aretai* for different stations and sexes. "If it is manly virtue you are after, it is easy to see that the virtue of a man consists in managing the city's affairs capably. . . . Or if you want a woman's virtue, that is easily described. She must be a good housewife, careful with her stores and obedient to her husband. Then there is another virtue for a child, male or female, and another for an old man, free or slave as you like, and a great many more kinds of virtue. . . . For every act and every time of life, with reference to each separate function, there is a virtue for each one of us . . . " (*Meno* 71e-72a). (Meno's list reflects the not-yet-completed transition from viewing arete as the performance of appropriate tasks to

---

[3]The following account of the concept of "Truth" is presented in Benjamin Daise, "The Will to Truth in Kierkegaard's Philosophical Fragments," *Philosophy of Religion* 31 (1992): 1-12.

the condition for performing those tasks well.) It is in the Socratic dialogues that the effort is made to identify the condition for performing well as a human being, and, specifically, man's arete, with wisdom or insight. Now, insofar as wisdom can be understood as a kind of knowledge,[4] it is understandable as "having the truth." Therefore, asking how far it is possible to teach the truth, as Climacus does, amounts to asking how far it is possible to teach human excellence or the ideal of self. That is why Climacus is able to identify his question with the "Socratic question" about virtue. That question is about the extent to which it is possible to teach what is essential to being a person.

The Questions of the Title Page

The Concept of "Eternal"

In the questions on the title page, the term "eternal" explicitly modifies "consciousness" and "happiness" and, implicitly, it modifies "interest." So, it is noteworthy that the concern addressed in the questions has to do with something explicitly related to a person. It is about a state or condition of an individual, not about eternity *per se*. The questions are not, without further ado, about consciousness *of* something that is eternal, but an eternal consciousness; not about an interest *in* something that is eternal, but an eternal interest; not about happiness *in* eternity, but eternal happiness. The concern is not, without further ado, metaphysical, but rather, anthropocentric.

The questions ask about a possibility, and that kind of question is only prompted if there is some *prima facie* reason for doubt. Here the two crucial concepts involved seem to be incompatible. That fact would tend to raise doubts about the possibility of a relationship between two things to which the concepts are separately applied. The assumption is that there is something problematic about a relationship between something historical and something eternal.

---

[4]In the argument for the teachability of virtue, the language is shifted from the use of *episteme* (knowledge) in the hypothesis to *phronesis* (wisdom). The significance of the shift seems to be to identify virtue with practical knowledge, with knowing the "right use" of things (*Meno* 88e).

The basis for the assumption is the operative understanding of the concepts of "the historical" and "the eternal." The relevant part of that understanding is articulated in the section called "Interlude." "Everything that has come into existence is *eo ipso* historical, for even if no further historical predicate can be applied to it, the crucial predicate of the historical can still be predicated—namely, that it has come into existence. . . . It is, however, the perfection of the eternal to have no history, and of all that is, only the eternal has absolutely no history" (PF 70-71). A necessary condition for applying the term "historical" to anything is that the thing has come into existence. A necessary condition for applying the term "eternal" to anything is that the thing has not come into existence. "But the historical is the past . . . " (PF 76). It is a dimension of temporality, and everything temporal is understood as subject to having the term applied to it. "[T]he present on the border of the future has not yet become historical . . . " (PF 76). That implies that the present, a temporal dimension, will become historical. "The future has not occurred as yet . . . " (PF 77), but its occurrence makes it present and eventually past. So the denial of a history for the eternal amounts to a denial of temporality. The problem with considering a relationship between the historical and the eternal, then, seems to be that the former is temporal and the latter is atemporal. Mutually exclusive conditions are necessary for them.

While this would seem to rule out applying the terms "historical" and "eternal" to the same thing, it does not automatically rule out a relationship between two things to which the terms are severally applied. There can be relationships between good and bad things, hot and cold things, and so on. The difference, of course, is that the terms "temporal" and "atemporal" would define entire spheres of existence, and the question of the possibility of a relationship concerns not just two items to which mutually exclusive predicates apply, but two whole realms. The issue posed is analogous to the traditional mind/body problem, which is constituted by the conjunction of four propositions that cannot be true together:

(1) The body is a material thing.
(2) The mind is an immaterial thing.
(3) Mind and body interact.
(4) Material and immaterial things cannot interact.

The issue here is constituted by conjoining the following (where X and Y are understood to be existent things):

(a) X is a temporal thing.
(b) Y is an eternal thing.
(c) X and Y are positively related.
(d) Temporal and eternal things cannot be positively related.

Proposed "solutions" to the mind/body problem deny one of the four propositions. "Idealism" denies (1). Materialism denies (2). Epiphenomenalism denies (3). Interactionist dualism denies (4).

Responses to the temporal/eternal relation run along similar lines. A Parmenides denies (a). The view that eternity is extension throughout all time effectively denies (b), insofar as "eternal" is understood as "atemporal." A proponent of (c) needs to overcome the considerations that lead to asserting (d). Those considerations are similar to the ones to be made on behalf of (4) in the mind/ body problem. Material things, it is said, are located in space, and in order for them to act on or be acted on by something, that something must be located in space. Immaterial things, it is said, are not located in space. Therefore, material and immaterial things cannot interact. Existence in the same realm is assumed to be a necessary condition for interaction. Similarly, temporal things are said to be in time. Eternal things are not. The two kinds of things lack a necessary condition for a positive relationship, existence in the same realm.

That assumption is challenged by Stump and Kretzmann with their notion of eternal/temporal simultaneity or ET-simultaneity.

> For every x and for every y, x and y are ET-simultaneous if
> (i) either x is eternal and y is temporal, or vice versa; and
> (ii) for some observer, A, in the unique eternal reference frame, x and y are both present—that is, either x is eternally present and y is observed as temporally present, or vice versa; and
> (iii) for some observer, B, in one of the infinitely many temporal reference frames, x and y are both present—that is, either x is observed as eternally present and y is temporally present, or vice versa.[5]

---

[5]Eleonore Stump and Norman Kretzmann, "Eternity," *Journal of Philosophy* 78/8 (August 1981): 439.

That notion is used to pave the way for other positive relationships between temporal and eternal things, such as acting on and being acted on. Even if this works, Stump and Kretzmann acknowledge that it would not be sufficient to solve the kind of problem presented by the idea of the Incarnation, that is, the *involvement* of something eternal in the temporal.

That is the kind of problem that is posed by the questions on the title page, even though, at first glance, it appears to be only a matter of a relationship that does not suppose involvement of the eternal in the temporal. As soon as it is noted, however, that the "eternal consciousness" referred to is a consciousness of (that is, that belongs to) a person, who is temporally located and that the (implicitly) eternal "interest" and (potential) "eternal happiness" also belong to a person, it becomes clear that the question asks about the possibility of involvement of the eternal in the temporal. That point is underscored in *Postscript* by Climacus's formulation of his response to the questions of the title page: "I, Johannes Climacus, born and bred in this city and now thirty years old, an ordinary human being like most folk, assume that highest good, called an eternal happiness awaits me just as it awaits a housemaid and a professor. I have heard that Christianity is one's prerequisite for this good. I now I ask how I may enter into relation to this [teaching, *Lære*] . . . [Christianity] wants be make the single individual eternally happy . . . " (CUP 16; SV 9, 18-19). Climacus locates himself spatially and temporally to underscore that it is that spatially and temporally located self that is interested in acquiring the eternal happiness.

While Climacus's point might be taken to highlight a metaphysical problem, the understanding of which would involve analysis of the concepts of "time" and "eternity," taking the point in that way would be to ignore some obvious signs in the very language used and some explicit pointers later in the work. The passage cited articulates an *interest* on the part of Climacus. It articulates an interest, not in the sense of something that simply arrests one's attention and is the object of curiosity. It articulates an interest in the sense that there is something at stake, that there is something of value involved. Climacus's articulated concern is for his "good" and not just any good, but his "highest good." So, the kind of interest articulated is the sort that is opposed to being *disin-terested* as distinct from *un*interested. Additionally, Climacus raises the question of what he must do in order to receive the good about which he is concerned. He asks how "I may enter into relation to this [teaching]." The expression of interest and the expectation of significance for action are signs that the problem addressed is not one for a disinterested, cognitive observer. The issue is not posed as a metaphysical question. That is the point Climacus makes throughout the text by his criticism of the "objective tendency."

The "objective tendency" is exactly what is represented by Meno's disinterested asking about *arete*, and Socrates' ironic response that makes fun of Meno is the model for Climacus. "The existing subject . . . ," Climacus says, "is existing, and so indeed is every human being. Yet let us not do the wrong of calling the objective tendency impious, pantheistic self-worship; but rather view it as a venture in the comic" (CUP 124). Given those clear indications, it would certainly be an essay in the comical to read the questions of the title page as metaphysical questions. Thus, if we are to avoid the comical, we need to ask just what the non-metaphysical concerns are that inhabit the questions that drive both *Fragments* and *Postscript*.

My procedure here is simple, even if it cannot be simply executed. It can be illustrated by a fairly simple example. Suppose you are stranded on an island and you notice a tornado headed your way. You ask if it is possible to get to a nearby island that you think is out of harms way. As the storm approaches, you struggle with the relationship between certain capacities you have and the proposed objective, and everything seems to point to the impossibility of achieving your aim. Suppose it turns out that on the island on which you are stranded, there is a place burrowed out in which you can take shelter. For someone to point that place out to you is not for that someone to respond literally to your question. It would, however, be for that someone to respond to the concern behind the question. Seeing what is accomplished by acting on what is pointed out is seeing what the concern was.

My suggestion is that *Fragments* and *Postscript* function like pointers away from some metaphysical island and to a burrowed place of refuge. We may come to understand the operative view of the concerns in them by seeing the direction in which they point and what might be accomplished by following them.

The Direction of *Fragments*

It has been noted that the un-Socratic view in *Fragments*, acknowledged in the last pages as Christianity, purports to present the very possibility asked about on the title page. How is it that the view sees that possibility as constituted? We should note first what is not done. Not a single ounce of intellectual effort is expended to show how the concepts of "eternity" and "temporality" are such that some manifestation of them might intersect. Instead, the view takes the intersection to have occurred and the intellectual challenge that is left is the wholly surmountable one of inferring the possibility from the actuality. Acceptance of the "fact" of the manifestation is not an intellectual challenge.

How can it be said that acceptance of the purported manifestation does not constitute an intellectual challenge when it is explicitly referred to not as just a paradox but as the "Absolute Paradox"? Is not paradox the ultimate in intellectual challenge and, consequently, is not the "Absolute Paradox" the quintessential intellectual challenge? In order to see why the "Absolute Paradox" is not presented as an intellectual challenge, we need to attend to what goes on around the use of that expression.

The story of the manifestation of the possibility in question is presented in chapter 2. It is presented as if conjured up by a poet to resolve a problem. How is the god, the would-be teacher, to accomplish the objective of becoming a teacher? Why is there a problem with that? According to the story, the god loves the would-be learner. "Yet this love is basically unhappy, for they are unequal, and what seems so easy—namely, that the god must be able to make himself understood—is not so easy if he is not to destroy that which is different" (PF 25). The "problem" is due to the fact of inequality.

But in what does the inequality consist? Unlike in the Socratic perspective which has the teacher and the learner both having the truth and, consequently, equal in that respect, in the un-Socratic alternative, the teacher has the truth and the learner does not. That is the inequality that is to be bridged—without "destroy[ing] that which is different." The would-be learner is a person, and the person is to become a being with the possibility of attaining the truth, without having his/her identity as person annihilated. The objective is to present this possibility, and according to the story, this is done by the teacher's becoming a person—with the truth. The challenge is to accept this person as the teacher.

The challenge in the story is certainly a prodigious one. But is it a challenge to the intellect, such that it deserves to be called a paradox? Is there anything paradoxical about a lover's desiring unity with the beloved? Is there anything paradoxical about a lover's doing what it takes to achieve unity with the beloved? Is there anything paradoxical about a person's having the truth? Is there anything paradoxical about the god's being a person? I submit that there is nothing paradoxical about any of those— without further ado. That further ado takes place in chapter 3 and is overlaid on the story. The "Absolute Paradox" is not in the story but overlaid on it. We need to see how it gets generated.

Just as in the two preceding chapters, Climacus begins chapter 3 with a brief recitation of the Socratic perspective. There was, he says, a Socratic paradox due to the fact that Socrates, supposedly the wisest of men and a student of human nature, declared himself to be ignorant of himself. What, exactly, is the paradox? We are aware of paradoxes attributed to Socrates in the Platonic corpus. No one does evil voluntarily. To know the good is to do the good. But the combined wisdom and ignorance of Socrates is explained in *Apology*. Socrates understood his wisdom to consist precisely in his awareness of his ignorance. He may be seen as superior in wisdom to others, who, though ignorant, entertain the conceit that they have knowledge. So the Socratic paradox of which Climacus speaks is not one that is spoken by Socrates, but one that involves Socrates. It is constituted by the relationship between Socrates, the wisest of men, and other men, and between Socrates and the truth. The wisest of men, who may be presumed to have the truth, lacks the truth. The Socratic paradox is, therefore, relative. Not only is it relative, the explanation given by Socrates shows that it is understandable.

By contrast, the paradox Climacus attributes to the un-Socratic perspective is to be absolute—not dependent on any relationship—and irresolvable. In what does this paradox consist? First of all, if it is to be absolute, it must be completely resistant to thought, and what is completely resistant to thought could be discovered to be that only by virtue of being aimed at by thought. Climacus gives an account of the occurrence of that.

> But the ultimate potentiation of every passion is always to will its own downfall, and so it is also the ultimate passion of the understanding [Forstand] to will the collision, although in one way or another the collision must become its downfall. This, then, is the ultimate paradox of thought: to want to discover something that thought itself cannot think. (PF 37)

This account deserves some scrutiny.

In the account, human capacities are personified. Passions and thoughts are spoken of as capable of willing. Climacus seems clear about the fact that he is personifying and not speaking literally. Earlier he had compared "the thinker without the paradox . . . [to] the lover without passion . . . " (PF 37). Thought is clearly the thought of a person who thinks and love and passion belong to a person who loves. So the willing that is attributed to the passions and to thought is the willing of a person. So, Climacus is presenting an abbreviated analogical argument in the account. Just as a particular will is operating in a person who has other passions, so is that will operating in a person whose passion is associated with thinking.

How might the argument look in fuller form? A person who fears wills the downfall of fear by willing the destruction of the feared object (or that the feared object in some other way be rendered impotent). A person who loves wills union with the beloved and thereby the elimination of the beloved as other and hence as an object of love. (Cf. the myth of androgyny in *Symposium*.) A person who dreads wills the definition of the object of dread and hence its transformation into an object of fear, at worst. Pity, jealousy, hatred, grief might be treated in the same way, giving support to the Climacian claim about the will associated with passions. (Joy is troublesome.)

The other part of the argument depends on the identification of some passion associated with thinking. Is there such a passion? In seeking an answer, we might note that in the first part of the argument constructed for Climacus, "passion" (*Lidenskab*) is understood as referring to emotions. (The term is also used in the section of the text under discussion in the sense of "excitement" when

Climacus speaks of the "lover without passion." Clearly, one cannot be a lover, in the sense of a person who loves, without passion, in the sense of the emotion.) In that part of the argument, emotions are understood as the manifestations of some desire. That understanding is expressed by Climacus's speaking about what the passions will. Depersonification yields the view that the person with the passion desires something and that the passion is the manifestation of that desire. So, when Climacus speaks of "the ultimate passion of the understanding," he is to be understood as meaning that there is some desire that is manifested in thinking. Our question is: What, if any, desire might that be?

On one level, the desire associated with thinking might be put quite simply. In thinking, a person aims at rendering known that which is unknown. In being known, the object of thought would be rendered unfit for investigation. (Meno asserted as much in the eristic dilemma.) Whether or not this is a real possibility is beside the point here, which is an understanding of the desire. Now, if we follow the lines suggested in the first part of the argument, we would have to say that the ultimate aim of thought is to render known everything that is unknown. Like the other passions, the downfall of which would come about through satisfaction of the desire, the downfall of thought that is willed in its "ultimate potentiation" would come through knowing everything that was unknown.

The conclusion Climacus reaches, then, depends on a flaw in the argument. Unlike the downfall of the other passions, which comes through satisfaction, the downfall of thought is to come through frustration. Thought wills to think something it *cannot* think. The other passions involve desiring something one *does not*, not *cannot*, have. The abbreviation of the argument conceals the flaw.

If we take the conclusion of the argument seriously, though, we would have to say that thought discovers a thought-resistant object. By thinking, we discover something that cannot be known. In accordance with what he has a right to claim by the argument, Climacus refers to this discovery of thought as the unknown (*det Ubekjendte*). The operative notion, however, is of the unknowable. "[I]t is the absolutely different in which there is no distinguishing mark" (PF 45). That is to say, what is merely unknown is distinguishable from what is known. There is at least some feature of it that allows you to say that this is not some other known thing. That distinguishing feature would be, of course, what might be used to later transform what is initially unknown into something known. To say that "there is no distinguishing mark" is to say that this possibility does not obtain. What is referred to is not just unknown, but unknowable.

Climacus whimsically assigns the name "the god" to the unknown. "But what is this unknown against which the understanding in its paradoxical passion collides and which even disturbs man and his self-knowledge? It is the unknown. But it is not a human being, insofar as he knows man, or anything else that he knows. Therefore, let us call this unknown the god. It is only a name we give to it" (PF 39).

Several points are noteworthy about the passage above. (1) The use of the expression "the god" underscores the fact that the perspective from which Climacus is speaking is the Greek perspective. That locution is not at home in Danish, but it is in Greek. ("In paganism God is regarded as the unknown" (P VIII-1 A 30). (2) While Climacus is speaking from a Greek perspective, he is trying to present the un-Socratic perspective. The assumption that man knows himself functions to negate the Socratic view, since Socrates declared that he did not know himself. (3) Calling the unknown "the god" calls to mind the meeting of the Greek perspective and Christianity when the apostle Paul said to the men of Athens, "What therefore you worship as unknown, this I proclaim to you" (Acts 17:23). Indeed, it is this meeting, this clashing of perspectives that is the collision of which Climacus speaks. It is this meeting that generates the "Absolute Paradox."

The "paradox" is initially identified as the assertion that the understanding comes to know something about the unknown, the absolutely different. Additionally, if the understanding is to know something about the unknown, it must first know that it is absolutely different. "If this is not immediately clear, then it will become more clear from the corollary, for if the god is absolutely different from a human being, then a human being is absolutely different from the god—but how is the understanding to grasp this? At this point we seem to be at a paradox" (PF 46). Climacus never explicitly says that the assertion I indicated is the paradox, but that is clear from the explanation that is given about what must hold for us to arrive at the paradox. "The understanding cannot come to know *this* by itself . . . if it is going to come to know this, it must come to this from the god" (PF 46; emphasis mine). The "this" refers to the assertion that the unknown is absolutely different. That is what we are said to stand before as a paradox.

Another look at the explanation is in order, however. If A and B are absolutely different, then either (1) one of them is incapable of bridging the difference between A and B and the other is not or (2) neither of them is capable of bridging the difference. If (1) then the difference is not absolute, since it is capable of being bridged. If (2) then the difference is not absolute, since A and B would share an incapacity. So the very idea of "absolute difference" is rendered incoherent.

The importance of this flaw in the development is the same as the importance of the flaw in the argument noted earlier. It underscores the fact that what is being presented here by Climacus is unable to stand on its own dialectical feet. It is consciously contrived as if it were an independently developed metaphysical version of the Christian story, when it is, in fact, dependent on it.

> Insofar as philosophy is mediation, it holds true that it is not complete before it has seen the ultimate paradox before its own eyes. This paradox is the God-man and is to be developed solely out of the idea, and yet with constant reference to Christ's appearance, in order to see whether it is sufficiently paradoxical, whether Christ's human existence does not bear the mark of his not being the *individual* human being in the profoundest sense, to what extent his earthly existence does not fall within the metaphysical and the aesthetic. (P IV C 84)

The completion of the contrivance consists in an explanation of how the unknown, the absolutely different, proceeds to bridge the difference. In order to provide the explanation, though, Climacus must first "imagine" the absolutely different. To do that he has recourse to the Greek idea of god—god as Aristotle's Unmoved Mover. "But the god needs no pupil in order to understand himself, and no occasion can act upon him in such a way that there is just as much in the occasion as in the resolution. When, then, moves him to make his appearance? He must move himself and continue to be what Aristotle says of him, ακινετος παντα κινει"

(PF, 24). God is completely self-sufficient and unchanging. This characterization clearly places the god outside the temporal world. The absolutely different becomes the absolutely equal in order to teach persons in what the absolute difference consists. Now, there is nothing in the initial characterization of the god on which to base the claim later made. In obvious reliance on the Christian story, the absolute difference is identified as sin. Consequently, a person's learning the difference would constitute consciousness of sin. The explanation is of how this could be taught.

> Only the god could teach it—if he wanted to be teacher. But this he did indeed want to be, as we have composed the story, and in order to be that, he wanted to be the equal of the individual so that he could understand him. Thus the paradox becomes even more terrible, or the same paradox has the duplexity by which it manifests itself as absolute. . . . (PF 47; SV 6, 46)

So the Absolute Paradox is the idea that the absolutely unlike is the absolutely equal, that the unbridgeable gap is bridged. It is the idea of the God-man.

It is clear that this paradoxical idea is paradoxical because it is self-contradictory.[6] The absolutely unlike becomes like. The abso-

---

[6]Stephen Evans argues as follows against the notion that the Absolute Paradox is a formal contradiction:

> [I]f the paradox is a formal contradiction and can be known to be such, the assumption that undergirds the B hypothesis of Philosophical Fragments, which is that human beings lack the Truth would be undermined. Those who assume that the incarnation is a logical contradiction believe that we have a clear understanding of what it means to be God and what it means to be a human being. God is infinite, eternal, all-knowing; human beings are finite, temporal, limited in their knowledge. Thus we can know that the predicates "God" and "human being are logically exclusive. All this assumes that we have a reliable, natural knowledge of both God and human beings. (C. Stephen Evans, *Passionate Reason: Making Sense of Kierkegaard's "Philosophical Fragments"* [Bloomington: Indiana University Press, 1992] 103.)

Evans is almost right. It is not that those who interpret the Absolute Paradox as a formal contradiction make the assumptions he mentions. It is, rather, that some of us acknowledge the assumptions with which Climacus operates in generating the story of the appearance of the Teacher. It is precisely the making of those assumptions that forms a part of the presumptuousness of the understanding that Climacus wants to take down a peg. Thus, to consider an earlier argument by Evans (102), when Climacus says that there is a distinction between

lutely unequal becomes equal. The unmoved moves. The unchanging enters the realm of the changing and behaves in the way other things in that realm behaves. If those alternative ways of characterizing the idea do not amount to contradiction, then nothing does.

Climacus indicates his awareness of the fact that the arguments and explanations offered on behalf of the uncovering of the paradox by the understanding do not work. He says about the view that the absolute difference is discovered and is resolved into likeness that it is "the self-ironizing of the understanding . . . " (PF 45). He is perfectly aware, as some critics of Kierkegaard have pointed out, that out of the idea of "absolute difference" no singular story of a God-man emerges.[7] In fact, he outlines a story that is different from the Christian story.

> There exists, then, a certain person who looks just like any other human being, grows up as do other human beings, marries, has a job, takes tomorrow's livelihood into account as a man should. It may be very beautiful to want to live as the birds of the air live, but it is not permissible, and one can indeed end up in the saddest of plights, either dying of hunger—if one has the endurance for that—or living on the goods of others. This human being is also the god. (PF 45)

If one takes seriously the idea of the God-man as simply generated by the idea of the unknown becoming known, of the nonhuman being human, this will do just as well as the story told in chapter 2 of *Fragments*. By assuming the perspective of the philosopher who attempts to generate Christianity "solely out of the idea," Climacus invites us to see the misconceptions, the erroneous think-

---

(a) the meaninglessness of self-contradiction in supposing that the god is god to the first generation and later generations are god to subsequent generations and (b) the meaninglessness of the idea of the incarnation, he is acknowledging what I have said. That is, that the Christian story itself contains no self-contradiction. It is not presented in *Fragments*, however, on its own terms. It is presented as intertwined with Greek or contemporary philosophical assumptions.

[7]Stephen Evans thinks that it is a problem for the view that the paradox is a logical contradiction "that it cannot explain what is 'absolute' or unique about the paradox of the incarnation" (Evans, *Passionate Reason*, 106). That would be a problem only if you took Climacus's account to be a serious and straightforward development of the Christian idea. It should be clear that Climacus does not see himself as engaged in that kind of account.

ing, and the presumptuousness needed for that project to seem to prosper.

Now, insofar as the "Absolute Paradox" is generated in the way that Climacus presents it, it is apparent that nothing in the Christian story alone is responsible for it. The starting point used for generating the "Absolute Paradox" is the identification of God as the unknown and, indeed, the unknowable. That identification is not a part of the Christian story. We get in the book of John, "For God so loved the world that he gave his only Son, that whoever believes in him should not perish but have eternal life" (John 3:16). We do not get God as the unknown and unknowable deciding to become man. That rendition was the product of Climacus's "poetical venture" in chapter 2 to connect the Socratic or Greek perspective with the un-Socratic alternative. The connection, as it turns out, amounts to a collision. The clashing of the view from the Greek perspective that God is the unknown with the view from the Christian perspective that God is manifested in the person of Christ is the "Absolute Paradox."

By presuming to represent Christianity as the product of thought, Climacus presents Christianity as absolutely paradoxical. Three points are to be noted in this connection. (1) By attending to this, we see another way in which Climacus's effort is a manifestation of the Socratic art. (2) By examining the point above, we see that the challenge presented by the "Absolute Paradox" is not an intellectual one. (3) In understanding the nature of the challenge presented by the "Absolute Paradox," we see what concern is addressed by it and *mutatis mutandis* what concern is addressed by the questions of the title page.

Paradox as Socratic Device

In "The Ways of Paradox," Quine distinguishes three kinds of paradoxes: (1) falsidical, (2) veridical, and (3) antinomous. A paradox is, etymologically, an idea or claim that is against (*para*) belief (*doxa*). However, a paradox is not just anything that is contrary to belief; a paradox is absurdly against belief. It is against belief that anyone might be expected to have. According to Quine's distinctions, a paradox may be due to a necessarily false assumption, such as the barber paradox. In a certain town, there is a man who shaves all and only those men who do not shave themselves. Who shaves the barber? The barber shaves himself, if and only if he does not shave himself. The problem with the story is that it assumes that there can be a town such as the one described and there cannot be. The paradox is a falsidical one.

Consider, alternatively, the following. There is a town in which the barber shaves all and only those men who do not shave themselves. Who shaves the barber? We seem to have the same paradox, but the air of absurdity vanishes if we say that the barber is a woman. What is said is true but its truth is obscured by the need of an explanation. The paradox is veridical.

There is also the kind of paradox that is an antinomy. One example of an antinomy that Quine gives is called Grelling's paradox. It concerns the adjectives "heterological" (not true of itself) and "autological" (true of itself). The paradox arises if we try to answer the question: Is "heterological" autological or heterological? If it is autological, then it is heterological, and if it is heterological, then it is autological. What are we to do with such a paradox? As Quine points out, we could be rid of the problem by refusing to use the locutions "true of" and "not true of." That remedy is more drastic than is needed, though, because the problem only arises in one special case, when "heterological" is applied to itself. The problem is resolvable by foregoing the self-referential usage.

While Grelling's paradox may seem trivial, it is not, for it is illustrative of how antinomous paradoxes arise and may be resolved. The problem arose from following a rule that we generally follow and assume that we can follow without restriction. The rule is that we may define terms and employ them meaningfully without restriction. The paradox is the stimulus to look at that assumption and get rid of it. The same kind of situation may arise with respect to other assumptions that operate in our view of the world. "An antinomy . . . packs a surprise that can be accommodated by nothing less than a repudiation of part of our conceptual heritage."[8]

The Quinean lesson about antinomies is actually an old Kantian lesson. Kant's consideration of the "Antinomy of Pure Reason" involves the posing of four questions. (1) Does the world have a

---

[8]W. V. O. Quine, *The Ways of Paradox* (New York: Random House, 1968) 11.

beginning in time and is it spatially limited? (2) Is there a simple thing out of which composite things are made? (3) Is there freedom in the world? (4) Is there a necessary being that is the cause of the world? For each of those questions Kant constructs two *reductio* arguments, one concluding with an affirmative answer and one concluding with the negative answer. Part of the lesson to be gained from the exercise is that the conflicts arise when we suppose that any question that we pose admits of an answer that can be arrived at by rational effort. That assumption about the limitless employability of reason must be discarded if we are to avoid antinomy.

The general lesson is one that is operating in the Socratic maneuvers. It recognizes the stimulative function of paradox and uses it to incite just the kind of self-examination that resolution requires. The operation of the procedure in the construction of paradox is, however, only the culturally generalized form of what takes place in the Socratic elenchus. When, for example, Socrates questions Euthyphro about the nature of piety, he asks Euthyphro if he believes the stories about the gods (*Euthyphro* 6b). Those stories portray the gods as fighting among themselves and otherwise behaving in supremely human ways. The reason for the question is that Euthyphro had advanced the thesis that piety is what the gods love. So, if Euthyphro believes the stories, there is a problem with his using the principle he advanced for determining if something is pious, since the fighting among the gods shows that they love different things (*Euthyphro* 8a). The problem is resolvable by Euthyphro's giving up one of the beliefs in question.

Giving up a belief is not the only way Euthyphro's conflict can be resolved, however. It is possible that the idea of piety as what the gods love might be clarified in such a way that the problem disappears. Indeed, this is the strategy Euthyphro adopts when he, effectively, moves to the position that piety is what all the gods love (*Euthyphro* 8b), and Socrates formulates the position explicitly for him. "But suppose that we now correct our definition, and say what the gods all hate is unholy, and what they love is holy . . . " (*Euthyphro* 9d). This conflict, then, resembles the veridical paradox. It is not so deeply rooted in the conceptual apparatus that it cannot be explained away. Given the explanation, the difficulty disappears. The exposure of conflict is what stimulates self-examination.

The conflict exposed by the arguments concerning the teach-ability of virtue in *Meno* is deeply rooted in Athenian thinking. Socrates' articulation of the conflict amounts to his constituting an antinomous paradox that belongs to Athenian thought. The function of formulating, presenting, and leaving it unresolved is to challenge the audience to engage in the kind of self-reflection that might bring resolution. The paradox presents unfinished business. Paradoxes, Kierkegaard wrote, are nothing but "undeveloped grandiose thoughts" (P II A 755).

The Nature of the Challenge

What exactly is the challenge presented by the "Absolute Para-dox" in *Fragments*? We have seen that the "Absolute Paradox" is constituted by the combination of a view of God that belongs to Greek philosophy and the view of God found in Christianity. But, as we have seen, an antinomous paradox can only be accommodat-ed by "repudiation of part of our conceptual heritage." What is the cash value of such a repudiation in this case? What kind of conse-quence attaches to meeting the challenge? We have already seen what kind of consequence might be expected from the paradox in *Meno*.

In *Meno*, the conflict is between the view that virtue is some-thing that is teachable and the view that it is not teachable. The former view presupposes that virtue is a kind of knowledge and is, therefore, a proper object of inquiry. Meno's putting forth the eristic dilemma was, effectively, a denial of the view that virtue can be acquired through inquiry. The recollection story and the slave boy demonstration aimed at dislodging Meno's initial view. The anticipated effect of success was "that we shall be better, braver and more active men . . . " (*Meno* 86c). The challenge was not, then, a primarily intellectual one, but one aimed at changing the person fundamentally. It aimed at changing Meno's orientation towards himself and the rest of the world.

The story and demonstration met with only limited success, as we saw, and the paradox constituted by the arguments on the teachability of virtue aimed at forcing confrontation with the need for fundamental change. The fact that the anticipated change would be not primarily intellectual but life-practical is underscored at the very end of the dialogue with an explicit challenge to Meno.

"[A]nd my request to you is that you will allay the anger of your friend Anytus by convincing him that what you now believe is true. If you succeed, the Athenians may have cause to thank you" (*Meno* 100b). The request assumes a change in *Meno*. Even though that change would involve seriously undertaking intellectual activity, the fundamental change is not itself an intellectual act. It is fundamentally a life-orientational change that is seen as appropriately manifested in different behavior, which is to include inquiry. It is change that is seen as behavior that is potentially effective in changing others and as potentially beneficial for the society at large.

Similarly, the challenge presented by the "Absolute Paradox" is one in which the outcome may be a radical change in a person. What, though, is the nature of that change? If it is not primarily an intellectual one, why does Climacus refer to the response called for as the "downfall" and the "stepping aside" of the understanding? Let us recall that what the god is to do is to present the truth to the learner, the condition for realization of oneself as a person, which condition the learner previously lacked. Thus, the difference in the learner prior to and after the appearance of the god is the change effected by a response to the paradox and is the manifestation of the essential condition. The difference is the something new that is brought by the teacher.

But what is the something new? The teacher is a person, and if there is something new, it must be in the way that the teacher is a person. How was it with him? "He went his way unconcerned about administering and distributing the goods of this world; he went his way as one who owns nothing and wishes to own nothing, as unconcerned about house and home as someone who has no hiding place or nest and is not looking for such a place" (PF 56). He lived a life motivated by love (PF 32-33) and aimed at love (PF 56). That understanding of self that is manifested in a life of love is the novelty. That understanding of self is also the ideality. Climacus is explicit about this. "All this [kind of life] seems very beautiful, but is it also proper? Does he not elevate himself above what is valid (*gjeldene*) for a human being?[9] Is it right for a human being to be as carefree as the bird and not fly hither and thither for food as the bird does? Should he not even think of tomorrow? . . . The question is this: May a human being express the same thing?—for otherwise the god has not realized the essentially human. Yes, if he is capable of it, he may also do it" (PF 56-57; SV 6, 54). What could be clearer? By living the way described, the god realizes the essential-human, and living that way is precisely the difference. So living that way is what constitutes the essential-human. A person "may also do it." It is possible for a person and, as "proper," it is incumbent on a person as a person.

To underscore the point that what is being offered as new is not something intellectual in character, immediately after characterizing the new ideal, Climacus sarcastically contrasts it with the work of those engaged in intellectual activity.

> This exalted absorption in his work will already have drawn to the teacher the attention of the crowd, among whom the learner presumably will be found, and such a person will presumably belong to the humbler class of people, for the wise and the learned will no doubt first submit sophistic questions to him, invite him to colloquia or put him through an examination, and after that guarantee him a tenured position and a living. (PF 57)

To see why adoption of that understanding of self might be seen as involving the downfall or setting aside of the understanding, we need only ask ourselves what it is that we expect of a rational person? How do we conduct our lives if we are to be considered rational and respectable? We go to school, plan a curriculum that will ensure gainful employment, get a job, save and invest, buy a house in the right area, marry the right person. That is the way of success and happiness. That is what everything in

---

[9]Swenson's translation of *gjeldene* as "valid" is preferable to Hong's translation of it as "ordinarily." The question of whether or not what the Teacher does is beyond what is ordinary is irrelevant to the concerns being addressed. The immediately preceding question makes the concern clear: Is the life in question *proper*? The question immediately after asks if that kind of life is *right* for a person. Those are questions of *validity*. Those are questions about a norm, not questions about a fact. Asking about whether the life is above what is ordinary is a factual kind of question.

our environment tells us. Meeting the challenge of the "Absolute Paradox," then, involves the overthrowing of that view of self based on our understanding of what rationality requires. But that is no intellectual matter. That addresses our fundamental stance towards ourselves and our world. It includes assigning a role to the intellect in the conduct of our lives. That role, however, is not the leadership role envisioned in Plato, Aristotle, or Aristotle's nineteenth century incarnation in Hegel. That is the sense in which the paradox calls for the downfall of the understanding.

The language that I use here—view of self, understanding of self—may seem to some to be in conflict with the claim that I make that what is at issue is not intellectual in character. Taking the language that way, however, ignores the fact that the language is not only used in that way. Consider the following question: "Are you an American?" That question asked at a border crossing requires an understanding of the concept 'American' and a knowledge of whether or not one meets the sufficient conditions for having the concept apply to one. It requires a response that is essentially cognitive.

The question "Are you an American or not?" asked during some international athletic competition or military situation, calls for some self-affirmation, a determination to behave in ways that bring credit to America or that uphold the values associated with America. It is like asking: Are you a man or a mouse? The response sought is not a cognitive one. It is one that affirms a sense of what one is. The question is indirect communication and asks for a response that is a doing.

That is the kind of response that the Absolute Paradox calls for. To say that it invites a different self-understanding is not to say that it invites some intellectual modification. Getting rid of the understanding is not a matter of changing the understanding in the sense of adopting some new cognitive position. It is affirming a self-understanding in which the intellect is not seen as the essential-constituting feature. Instead, a view of self as in loving solidarity with others is affirmed. So, it is a modification of the whole self in which the *place* of the intellect is altered, as distinct from merely altering some element of the intellect.

In order for that kind of response to be invited, the story of the Teacher needed to be told in the process. One can, of course, respond by asking whether or not this is the real story, or if the story is true, or if the Paradox is above the reason or against it, and so on. That is like the recruit's responding to the officer by saying you just have to tell me, when told that he is not talk under threat of force.

The Significance of the Question

The un-Socratic alternative presents itself as the basis for answering in the affirmative to the questions of the title page. "As is well known, Christianity is the only historical phenomenon that despite the historical—indeed, precisely by means of the historical—has wanted to be the single individual's point of departure for his eternal consciousness, has wanted to interest him otherwise than merely historically, has wanted to base his happiness on his relation to something historical" (PF 109). What, though, is the nature of the concern that is presupposed by the kind of response given? How is it that doing what meeting the challenge of the "Absolute Paradox" requires would address some concern? Identification of the concerns addressed would amount to identification of the concerns presupposed.

The prescription attached to the "Absolute Paradox" calls for a radical reorientation of oneself in such a way as to unbind oneself from one's selfish concerns and strive for solidarity with others. The prescription is for a life of love. We may understand the concern presupposed by this prescription as being either for release from the prior kind of life, which would have been a life of essential estrangement from others, or for something in relation to which the new kind of life would be a means. In other words, the new life could be understood as constitutive of what is aimed at in the search for "eternal happiness" or it could be understood as only a condition for what is aimed at in the search for "eternal happiness," with eternal happiness as something to be attained only after earthly life is over. Determining which of those two ways of understanding the new life applies would determine what the concern of *Fragments* is.

Chapter 3

The Concern of *Fragments*

The Key Concepts

Pascal complained about Descartes that "[i]n all his philosophy he would have been quite willing to dispense with God. But he had to make Him give a fillip to set the world in motion; beyond this, he has no further need of God" (*Pensees* #77). He also remarks that "[t]he God of the Christians is not a God who is simply the author of mathematical truths, or of the order of the elements; that is the view of heathens and Epicureans. . . . But the God of Abraham, the God of Isaac, the God of Jacob, the God of Christians, is a God of love and of comfort, a God who fills the soul and heart of those whom he possesses . . . " (*Pensees* #555). One could take Pascal to mean that there are different beings, one referred to in the Bible and another referred to in philosophical treatises. Alternatively, one can understand Pascal to mean that the concept "God" has different functions in a religious tradition (in regulating personal life) and in philosophical discourse (in explaining the fundamental nature of what there is). If one takes the latter view, one can understand Pascal as including the philosophical functions and religious functions under the same concept or as seeing the two kinds of functions as constituting different concepts. Whatever Pascal's view is, if the last alternative mentioned is correct, it would obviously result in massive confusion simply to fuse the two usages. I have contended that *Fragments* takes the last view, that it is directed at the confusion-making fusion just mentioned and that what is referred to as the "Absolute Paradox" is the culmination of that confusion.

The un-Socratic alternative presented in *Fragments* makes no mention of any special ontological realm in which what is aimed at is attainable. It makes no mention of any otherworldly state of affairs in which the desire for an "eternal happiness" is satisfied.

It makes no mention (except by way of comparison) of a supra-natural being with a cosmological mission. ("Oh, to sustain heaven and earth by an omnipotent 'Let there be,' and then, if this were absent for one fraction of a second, to have everything collapse—how easy this would be compared with bearing the possibility of the offense of the human race when out of love one became its savior!" [PF 32].) Nonetheless, the language that is usually linked to those kinds of ideas is used without any indication of blushing. "God," "the eternal," "faith" play key roles in the view that is presented. Are we to understand those terms to have some otherworldly significance even though the author does not explicitly assign any such significance to them? That is to say, are "God" and "the eternal" ontological peculiarities, the grasping of which requires an epistemological peculiarity called "faith"? Or should they be understood in some other way?

There has been no shortage of critics, both sympathetic and unsympathetic to Kierkegaard, who have opted for the former.[1] The old dispute about whether the "Absolute Paradox" is against the reason or above the reason has given way to the dispute about whether or not the concept of "faith" in *Fragments* presaged the "new epistemology,"[2] in which a subjective component is seen as legitimate. Both sides of both disputes agreed on the ontological significance of the language and argued about the epistemological respectability of its use.

What we have seen so far should at least cast doubt on the assumption operating in the debate. What is needed is an exploration of the significance of the language in question. The need for elasticity in interpretation was acknowledged by Kierkegaard at an early stage. He wrote:

> It is with the concept "Orthodoxy" as with the concept "Consistency"; many think that the latter consists in constantly doing the same thing and probably in such a way that [they

---

[1]See N. H. Søe, "Kierkegaard's Doctrine of the Paradox," in *A Kierkegaard Critique*, ed. H. Johnson and N. Thulstrup (Chicago: Henry Regnery, 1962).

[2]See C. Stephen Evans, "Kierkegaard and Plantinga on Belief in God: Subjectivity as the Ground of Properly Basic Religious Beliefs," *Faith and Philosophy* 5/1 (January 1988).

think that] if one carries an umbrella in rainy weather, one should also carry it in sunshine. (P I A 45)

If the very concept of "orthodoxy" is to be read as having some flexibility, then certainly the concepts operating within orthodoxy are to be viewed in the same way. Charting the connections among the network of concepts in which "eternal happiness" has a place may be possible by beginning with the central notion—the God-idea.

The God-Idea

A clear indication of the divergence from traditional philosophical theology in the Climacian writings is the short-shrift treatment given to arguments for the existence of God in *Fragments*. One of the reasons given for the cursory treatment is that the arguments involve a misunderstanding of the very concept of "God." The assertion of that misunderstanding is deceptively brief and bears examination. "God," Climacus says, " is not a name, but a concept (Begreb) . . . " (PF 41). In *Postscript*, Climacus uses the term *Fore-stilling* (translated as "idea" or "conception") rather than Begreb. *Forestilling* is also used by Anti-Climacus in *Sickness unto Death*. That distinction in usage is not significant enough to warrant mention in those texts. However, Climacus regards the distinction between "name" and "concept" as sufficiently significant to note.

What is the distinction between "name" and "concept" for Climacus? Specifically, what is the import of his remark that God is not a name but a concept? Unfortunately, Climacus does not say anything about what he understands the distinction to be. It is reasonable to suppose that he understands a name to be something like what Kripke aims at in calling a name a "rigid designator." "Let's call something a rigid designator if in every possible world it designates the same object."[3] Obviously, ordinary proper names do not succeed in making exclusive designations. There are hundreds of men named John Smith. Naming is, nonetheless, a device for referring to some specific object. There are other devices, such as definite descriptions, for performing the same kind of

---

[3]Saul A. Kripke, *Naming and Necessity* (Cambridge MA: Harvard University Press, 1980) 48.

operation. It is reasonable to attribute that understanding of "name" to Climacus, because it captures the ordinary view of a name as labelling an object. "London Bridge" labels a particular structure even if it is not in London. "Santa Claus" labels a particular imaginary person. So, even without understanding Climacus's view of what a concept is, we can see something of great significance in the distinction made by seeing what is denied. In Climacus's view, "God" does not pick out some object, not some real object, not some imaginary object.

It is noteworthy that in making the distinction in question, Climacus drops the locution ("the god") that he uses to represent the Greek perspective. The definite article in that expression suggests a referring function. (We can make no inference from the use of capital letters, since all nouns were capitalized in Danish and Greek.) Climacus's remark, made in connection with his criticism of arguments for the existence of God, suggests that those arguments, in which "God" is treated as a name, revert to the Greek perspective. It suggests that those arguments are not consistent with the un-Socratic alternative presented.

Understanding what Climacus denies when he says that God is not a name but a concept does not tell us what he is asserting. Just as it is the case that Climacus does not tell us how he uses the term "name," he does not tell us how he uses "concept."

John Whittaker provides a helpful discussion of the distinction considered here. He suggests, " By a 'name' Kierkegaard evidently means a proper name. A name refers to an individual as such, not as an instance of a description which might just as well be filled by other individuals."[4] This points to Whittaker's understanding of concept. "By a 'concept' Kierkegaard obviously meant some type of expression which does not designate its referent in any immediate way. Concepts acquire their reference only through some mediating descriptions, descriptions which identify what comes under those concepts. These descriptions define a concept by telling us what counts as its referent(s)" (Whittaker, 123-24). This account of the distinction between name and concept operates with an

---

[4]See John Whittaker, "Kierkegaard on Names, Concepts, and Proofs for God's Existence," *International Journal for the Philosophy of Religion* 10 (1979): 119.

unwarranted assumption, namely, that all concepts have referents. Some concepts clearly do have referents, but concepts such as love, justice, and the like do not.[5] There clearly is more to understanding how "concept" functions and possibly how it functions in Kierkegaard's works.

Since there is no indication that the term is used in any way that is peculiar to the perspective of the pseudonymous author of *Fragments*, we may look to the use of the term elsewhere in the authorship for suggestions. The term is used in the title of Kierkegaard's master's thesis, *The Concept of Irony*, and in the book pseudonymously authored by Vigilius Haufniensis, *The Concept of Anxiety*. Additionally, a number of works explicitly attempt to understand different "concepts." One place that is particularly instructive to consider is *Either/Or* I, where the concept of "sensuous erotic genius" is explored.

> Hence, we do not find the sensuous as a principle [*Princip*] in Greek culture; neither do we find the erotic as a principle based upon the principle of the sensuous. . . .
> So it was Christianity that posited sensuality as a principle, just as it posited the sensuous-erotic as a principle. The idea of representation [*Repræsentationens Idee* =the representation of the idea] was introduced into the world by Christianity. If I now imagine the sensuous-erotic as a principle, as a power, as a domain, defined in relations to spirit— that is defined in such a way that spirit excludes it—if I imagine this principle concentrated in a single individual, then I have the concept [*Begrebet*] of sensuous-erotic genius. . . . (EOI 64; SV 2, 62)

What is of import in that passage is the fact that "concept" is used interchangeably with "principle" and "idea." As such, it is understood as something that may be "excluded" by another principle, in this case spirit.

A explicitly states that "[t]he basic concept of man is spirit" (EOI 65). "Menneskets Begreb er Aand . . . " (SV 2 63). He is not

---

[5]The distinction as drawn by Whittaker is sufficient for his purposes, which is to explain something about Climacus's critique of arguments for the existence of God. Those arguments do treat God as a concept in the way that Whittaker explains it, that is, as an abbreviation of a set of descriptions—creator of the world, ruler of the world, etc. That does not mean, however, that the account fully captures Climacus's understanding.

claiming that the phenomenon of sensuousness did not obtain among the Greeks. He is saying that it was not there as something opposed by anything else. It was an integral part of the Greek culture, as he puts it, "it is posited not as a principle but as a consonant *encliticon*" (EOI 62). That is to say, it was absorbed into the whole and not distinguishable as something separate, the way Danish definite articles become a part of the noun when the noun is unmodified. For example, the word for *sun* is *sol*, but *the sun* is *solen*. "Concept" is, thus, understood not just as a principle for organizing experience but also as regulative. Christianity, according to A, grants status as a concept to sensuousness by becoming a competitor for ruling a life. So, "concept" includes the idea of a regulative principle.

When "concept" is understood in this way, it is understood in the way its German cognate, *Begriff*, is used by Hegel. In Hegel, *Begriff* is an indwelling urge in things that guides their development. It is the ideal that defines each thing as that sort of thing. It is this idea to which the pseudonymous editor of *Either/Or* calls attention with his opening sentence: "It may at times have occurred to you, dear reader, to doubt somewhat the accuracy of that familiar philosophical thesis that the outer is the inner and the inner is the outer" (EOI 3). We need to attend, then, to the way the concept of "God" is used in *Fragments* to see if that is the way it functions and not simply assume that it is simply a descriptive term that may or may not capture some actual phenomenon. If the use of "concept" in *Fragments* is like its use in *Either/Or*, then we would have to view Climacus's assertion that God is not a name but a concept as the claim that God is not an object, about which it makes sense to ask whether or not it is existent, but a principle about which it makes sense to ask whether or not it will guide one's life. These observations are merely suggestive. What needs to be done is to examine the employment of the expressions "God" and "the god" by Climacus.

I have argued that the Absolute Paradox is generated by fusing claims about God that are associated with different perspectives—the Greek philosophical view and the Christian view. That fusing was signalled in the opening question of the first chapter, as I have shown. Extracting some understanding of the way the concept "god" functions in a text that engages in that kind of mingling of views presents a challenge. It is especially difficult when the Greek view itself contains conflict of its own. (There are nine uses of "God" and one hundred fifty-seven uses of "the god." Of the nine uses of "God" two are uses with the indefinite article and one is a use with the definite article followed by an adjective.)[6] (*The Kierkegaard Indices* 2:369, 428-30.)

We may begin with the earliest (beyond the preface) use of the term, where it is clearly nestled in the Greek view. It is, after all, an exposition of what Climacus understands to be the Socratic view, which Climacus understands to be illustrative of the Greek perspective. Climacus says, "Socrates elaborates on this idea [that the learner already has the truth], and in it the Greek pathos is in fact concentrated, since it becomes a demonstration for the immortality of the soul" (PF 10). (A footnote to this passage observes that "this Greek idea is repeated in ancient and modern speculation." Thus, we are alerted in another way that the fusing of the Greek view with Christianity, resulting in the misunderstanding that Climacus presents, is not a Climacian invention, but a representation of current thinking.) The first two references to "god" are accompanied by supporting text from Plato. "Socrates, however, was a midwife examined by the god himself. The work he carried out was a divine commission (see Plato's *Apology*). . . . And the divine intention, as Socrates understood it, was that the god forbade him to give birth (μαιευσεσθαι με ο θεος αναγκαζει, γενναν δε απεκωλυσεν [the god constrains me to serve as a midwife, but has debarred me from giving birth], *Theaetetus*, 150c) . . . " (PF 10-11). (The bracketed passage is in the Hong translation.) The use of the term here is no different from its use in popular culture. Gods were beings capable of intervening in human affairs. They placed demands on humans to behave in accordance with their wishes, which had to be discerned somehow.[7] Socrates' statements about how the god affected him are not, at first glance, of special philosophical significance. It is by virtue of reflection on the kind of

---

[6]This comparison of the use of the two locutions suggests the pervasiveness of the Greek perspective in the text.

[7]See Joint Association of Classics Teachers, *The World of Athens: An Introduction to Classical Athenian Culture* (Cambridge: Cambridge University Press, 1984) 2.21–2.25.

claim Socrates makes that some understanding of the concept of "god" can be forged. That reflection for the Greeks is begun in the Platonic corpus, though, and culminates in Aristotle. Thus, it is not a peculiarly Climacian undertaking to draw the conclusions that are presented as an understanding of "the god."

What does it mean that Socrates is able to turn inward to find out if the way he proposes to proceed is sanctioned by the god? How can he get an answer to his question unless the god has somehow lodged it in him? If the god has somehow lodged the answer in him, does that not mean that the god is effectively in him? That this is the case is certainly the inference that Plato has his Socrates begin to make. Consequently, what is initially language that is not discrepant with popular usage comes to have significance not entertained in popular thought.

One aspect of this transformation is apparent as early as *Euthyphro*. We saw earlier that in response to Euthyphro's assertion that piety is what the gods love (7a), Socrates asks questions that lead Euthyphro to admit that the stories about the gods tell of fighting among them (7b-8a) and that if that is so the gods are not one with respect to what they love. Euthyphro, consequently, modifies his position to say that piety is what all the gods love (9e). While this view does not ultimately stand, the effect of that small exchange and that small change is the transformation of notions about the gods such that with respect to matters of piety, that is, with respect to what is of religious significance, the gods are, effectively, one. Thus, it makes sense to speak of the god, rather than the gods.

How, though, are we to ascertain what is right and wrong? When that question is addressed in *Crito*, Socrates argues that we should not heed what is said by the many, but only the one with expert knowledge. (48a) Now, it may or may not have escaped Plato that in order to ascertain that someone has expert knowledge in matters of right and wrong, one would have to have expert knowledge oneself. In any case, the implication of the view expressed in *Crito* is that one ought to heed oneself in determinations of right and wrong. To be sure, in *Republic*, it is supposed that the class of persons with expert knowledge is not all-inclusive and that some ought to take orders from others. Those who are understood as experts, however—the philosophers—are said to be "godlike" (500d). Even while maintaining the elitist position, Plato seems to hold that this divine rational nature is something universal. "But our present discussion . . . shows that the power to learn is present in everyone's soul" (*Republic* 518c). "[I]t is better for everyone to be ruled by divine reason, preferably within himself and his own, otherwise imposed from without" (*Republic* 590d). In *Meno*, though, one of the dialogues cited by Climacus, before Plato gets to that elitist position, the possibility of everyone's coming to learn everything is illustrated by the use of the slave boy in the "demonstration" of recollection. Thus, ascertaining the truth—what the god would have us do—is a matter of looking inward for everyone. The god is no externality, to which one is to turn to find guidance. As Climacus puts it in the second reference to god, "In the Socratic view, every human being is himself the midpoint, and the whole world focuses only on him because his self-knowledge is God-knowledge" (PF 11).

What Plato has done is to articulate a view that was implicitly held as early as Parmenides. In his prose poem, Parmenides tells of his passage from darkness to light. He speaks of being guided by goddesses on his journey. The culmination of that journey is represented as a kind of self-fulfillment. When we look at the literal basis for the claims that Parmenides makes that constitute the content of his Truth, we find that it is the work of reason that leads him there. It is by analyzing the concept of "being" that Parmenides concludes that what is cannot change, is unitary, and eternal.[8] That is to say, Parmenides infers the nature of what is from his understanding of a concept. So, it is reason that is the divinity that guides him to enlightenment.

This Parmenidean outlook is not lost on Plato, who adopts the Parmenidean predicates of "Being" in his theory of Forms. In *Theaetetus*, when Plato's Socrates subjects his predecessors to criticism for acceptance of the "knowledge is perception" thesis, he pointedly excepts Parmenides. "In this matter let us take it that, with the exception of Parmenides, the whole series of philosophers agree—Protagoras, Heraclitus, Empedocles . . . " (152e). The defer-

---

[8]See Charles Kahn, "The Greek Verb 'to be' and the Concept of Being," *Foundations of Language* (1966): 255.

ence to Parmenides is in effect, also, in the identification of the philosopher as god-like, as previously mentioned. There is explicit identification of reason with the divine, as well. "[T]he virtue of reason seems to belong to something more divine" (*Republic* 518e). "Fine things are those that subordinate the beastlike parts of our nature to the human—or better, perhaps, to the divine" (*Republic* 589d).

This same view—that rational nature is god-like—is present in Aristotle's *Metaphysics*. The identification of man's *physis* as the desire to get knowledge (*Metaphysics* 980a22), coupled with the identification of god as pure thinking (*Metaphysics* 1072b 19-29) effectively takes man's essence, the reason, to consist in the potential for divinity. Aristotle does not leave it for us to make an inference about this connection between man's *physis* and divinity in his thought, however. He directly addresses the question of whether the wisdom aimed at in thinking "may with some justification be regarded as not suited to man" (*Metaphysics* 982b 28). He responds by saying that "[t]he most divine knowledge is also most worthy of honor. This science alone may be divine, and in a double sense: for a science which God would most appropriately have is divine among the sciences; and one whose object is divine, if such there be, is likewise divine. Now our science has precisely these two aspects: on the one hand, God is thought to be one of the reasons for all things and to be in some sense a beginning; on the other hand, this kind of science would be the only kind or the most appropriate kind for God to have" (*Metaphysics* 983a5-10).

Climacus's observation, then, that in the Socratic view self-knowledge is knowledge of the god captures the idea that the god is in a person.[9] The idea that there is a potentiality for something

---

[9]In *Republic*, Plato is aware of the difference between the views put forth there as expressions of what is divine and popular religious views. He is also aware of the power of popular religion. Thus, after the proposal is made for governance of the city based on what can be ascertained by reason, the following exchange takes place:

What is now left for us to deal with under the heading of legislation?

For us nothing, but for the Delphic Apollo it remains to enact the greatest, finest, and first of laws.

What laws are those?

lodged in a being whose actual condition is incompatible with the realization of that potentiality is problematic. There is also the question of how persons are to be understood essentially in this view. Is self-realization to be understood as consisting in some activities/experiences in the temporal world? The dominant line of argument in *Republic* certainly takes that view. It is argued that the soul is made up of three parts, and the task of a person is to allow the rational part to rule (436A-442b). Or is self-realization to be understood as attainment of a state of affairs impossible in this world? Is the soul essentially the rational part alone? That possibility is also entertained. "We must realize what it [the soul] grasps and longs to have intercourse with, because it is akin to the divine and immortal and what always is, and we must realize what it would become if it followed this longing with its whole being, and if the resulting effort lifted it out of the sea in which it now dwells, and if the many stones and shells (those which have grown all over it in a wild, earthy, and stony profusion because it feasts at those so-called happy feastings on earth) were hammered off it. Then we'd see what its true nature is and be able to determine whether it has many parts or just one and whether or in what manner it is put together. But we've already given a decent account, I think, of what its condition is and what parts it has when it is immersed in human life" (*Republic* 611e-612a).

Thus, there is a version of the meeting of the divine and human as constituting a conflict that is wholly a product of Greek thinking. This Greek divinity of the human consists in understanding what is essentially human as something divorced from the world of everyday living. The conflict consists in seeing that something as inherent in and defining of the creature engaged in everyday living.

Those having to do with the establishing of temples, sacrifices, and other forms of service to gods, daimons, and heroes, the burial of the dead, and the services that ensure their favor. We have no knowledge of these things, and in establishing our city, if we have any understanding, we won't be persuaded to trust them to anyone other than the ancestral guide. And this god, sitting upon the rock at the center of the earth, is without a doubt the ancestral guide on these matters for all people. (427b-c)

The transformed understanding of "god" is at work in the third reference to god in the text. That reference is the one that captures Climacus's understanding of the Socratic view: "his self-knowledge is god-knowledge" (PF 11).

The next use of "god" occurs after Climacus has made a transition from discussing the Socratic view to discussing the radically un-Socratic view. Nonetheless, it is still with reference to the Socratic view. The first paragraph under the heading of "The Teacher" in the un-Socratic view reviews the Socratic situation, and the use in question occurs in that paragraph. Additionally, it is a nonspecific use of "god" and provides us no basis for coming to any understanding, except later by contrast. In the Socratic view, Climacus says, "the teacher is only an occasion, whoever he may be, even if he is a god" (PF 14). In the alternative view, the god is more than an occasion. The god provides the truth and the condition for receiving it. "[I]f it [reception of the condition and the truth] is to take place, it must be done by the god himself" (PF 15).

In the very next paragraph, "God" is used. It is significant that "God," not "the god" is used. This signals that the discussion is to be understood as about something other than the Socratic view, that is, that it represents a non-Greek perspective. In this context, it is said that if the teacher is to give the learner the truth "God must have given him [the Learner] the condition for understanding the truth (for otherwise he previously would have been merely animal and that teacher who gave him the condition along with the truth would make him a [person] for the first time" (PF 15).[10] Whatever else may be involved, "God" is a term here that is the equivalent of "person-maker."[11] Recall that in the Socratic view, even a god could not provide the truth, could not make a person.

---

[10]In this context, "person" is preferable to "human being" as a translation of *menneske*. "Human being" is a biological concept. "Person," on the other hand, has ethical significance.

[11]This term is ambiguous, to be sure. It could mean person-maker in the sense that there is an agent that constructs a person, or it could mean person-maker in the sense that there is a constitutive condition that comes to be. If the latter sense is understood, the obvious question for the philosopher is: What is the agent of the person-constituting? That is the obvious question for the philosopher. It is not a question that is addressed in the un-Socratic view.

In this un-Socratic view, person-making is precisely the function of God. That being the case, the Learner's deprivation of the condition could not have been due to god. This "inference" that Climacus draws from his hypothesis, thus, clearly depends on the operation of an understanding of "god" that is different from the one operating in the Greek view. Nonetheless, he continues to make use of the Greek locution, "the god." Not only is it used immediately before and after the use of "God," the opening sentences of the next two paragraphs repeat the Greek locution. The mingling of the different perspectives is signalled by the mingling of Greek and non-Greek locutions.

It is not only the case that the mingling takes place between sentences, it takes place within sentences. The Greek locution is used when the conception at work is clearly the non-Greek one. "The teacher is *the god* himself" (PF 15; my emphasis). "The teacher, then is *the god*, who gives the condition and gives the truth" (PF 15; my emphasis). This is where the real fusion takes place. That is, Climacus uses the expression "the god" in the sense of person-maker.

There is a difference to be noted in the uses of "God" and "the god" even in the midst of this mingling. "God" is used in the sense of original person-maker. The teacher, coming after the original constitution of the creature, is the new-person-maker and is referred to as "the god." That distinction in use is underscored in the tenth use of the term. "A teacher such as that, the learner will never be able to forget, because in that very moment he would sink down into himself again, just as the person did who once possessed the condition and then, by forgetting that God is, sank into unfreedom" (PF 17). Here, it is clear that it is consciousness of God that is essential for personhood. Whatever else God may be, this use is clear. God is that the consciousness of which is essential for personhood. The text uses "the god" to refer to the teacher as restoring the lost possibility of that consciousness. This mingling is to be understood in light of the project as one of indirect communication. Nonetheless, it is important to discern the constant function of the term. What constitutes the teacher is precisely the capacity to bring the possibility of self-realization to mankind.

This analysis is important for understanding Climacus's treatment of arguments for the existence of God. Given Climacus's view, those arguments are irrelevant to a proper relationship to God and indeed are obstructive.

> [S]o long as I am holding on to the demonstration (that is, continue to be one who is demonstrating), the existence does not emerge, if for no other reason than that I am in the process of demonstrating it, but when I let go of the demonstration, the existence is there. Yet this letting go, even that is surely something; it is, after all, meine Zuthat [my contribution]. Does it not have to be taken into account, this diminutive moment, however brief it is—it does not have to be long, because it is a leap. (PF 42-43)

As "God" is not a name that labels some object, the "leap" is not an act with epistemological significance, in which one comes to know some object or to know that some object exists. It is, rather, a giving up of the presuppositions that underpin the project of demonstration. Those presuppositions are ones that take oneself to be essentially related to God in some cognitive way. Those are presuppositions about what one is—about what it is to be a person.

Although there is much in Stephen Evans's analysis of "God" in the Climacian writings with which I agree, the conclusions I have just advanced are at odds with Evans's view. The reasons for the differences need consideration. At times, the view put forth by Evans seems almost identical to mine, but I suppose that at those times he sees himself as only representing one aspect of Climacus's understanding of God. He writes:

> Climacus himself certainly conceives of God in personal terms, and I believe that he thinks God is best conceived immanently in this way. . . . However, I do not think he holds that God must be conceived in such a form or that he is only known in this way. What is essentially known is the absoluteness, infinite demand, and eternal character of the moral law itself. God is essentially these characteristics.[12]

To say that "God is essentially these characteristics" of the moral law is to say that God is not some being that is distinct from the moral law. To say in the same breath, however, that God is

---

[12]C. Stephen Evans, Kierkegaard's "Fragments" and "Postscript": The Religious Philosophy of Johannes Climacus (Atlantic Highlands NJ: Humanities Press, 1983) 156.

conceived of "in personal terms," where that entails having the characteristics of a person, seems to me not to be representative of Climacus's view. Evans appears to use "in personal terms" in this sense. While the expression may mean "having significance to one as a person," Evans seems to use the expression in both senses. He says "that Climacus finds the most natural interpretation of moral obligation to be that moral obligation is a relation between persons. He himself experiences the moral 'ought' as a command, which therefore stems from a lawgiver and judge" (Evans, 157). The idea of God as referring to the absolute character of the moral law is close to—not the same as—the view I have advanced of God as a concept, where that is understood as a regulative principle. To be more precise, the view I put forth for the way God is used by Climacus is captured by what Kant calls "the ideal." "As the idea gives the rule, so the ideal in such a case serves as the archetype for the complete determination of a copy; and we have no other standard for our actions than the conduct of this divine man within us" (Kant, 486). It is not, to be sure, Climacus's view that this ideal is an ideal of reason. My point is simply about how the notion functions, not about its source. What would distinguish God as a regulative principle from other regulative principles would be its thoroughgoing and fundamental character. The idea of God as lawgiver and judge, however, employs "God" as a name, and Climacus explicitly denies that.

When God is understood as a concept and not as a name, God is not understood as playing a role in some cosmological scheme. So, it is important to avoid attributing metaphysical significance to remarks made by Climacus. We are given pointers to that effect in *Fragments* and explicit directions in *Postscript*. In chapter 2 of *Fragments*, the view departing from the Greek perspective presents God as teacher and savior. There is a brief contrast made between God viewed in that way and God viewed as a cosmological actor.

> Oh, to sustain heaven and earth by an omnipotent "Let there be," and then, if this were to be absent for one fraction of a second, to have everything collapse—how easy this would be compared with bearing the possibility of the offense of the human race when out of love one became its savior! (PF 32)

If one is tempted to interpret Climacus as comparing two divine tasks, it might be helpful to ask what basis there would be for seeing one thing as more difficult than another for God. The more plausible interpretation is that there is a comparison being made between the significance of God understood as playing a role in cosmology and God understood as playing a role in the governance of a person's life.

Although the passage above poses a qualitative difference between the two ways of understanding God, Evans sees the one view as leading to the other.

> Within this personal conception [of God] Climacus includes the traditional and overwhelmingly significant conception of God as creator. The ultimacy and absoluteness of morality and the individual's own sense of absolute responsibility toward God lead the individual to conceive of God as his creator and as the ruler of the universe. Though God is not directly present in nature, he is present there, and the individual who has acquired the requisite spiritual development can "see God everywhere." (Evans, KFP 157)

It would be helpful to look at the passage leading up to the phrase quoted by Evans.

> Nature, the totality of creation, is God's work, and yet God is not there, but within the individual man there is a possibility (he is spirit according to his possibility) that in inwardness is awakened to a God-relationship, and then it is possible to see God everywhere. (CUP 246-47)

Now, it is obvious that the language of "God as Creator" is used here, since nature is referred to as the "totality of creation." It is not clear, however, that the passage refers to a movement from the God-idea as essentially a spiritual relationship to the idea of God as Creator or to an enlargement of the God-idea to include the latter. The assumption involved in asserting the movement is that "see[ing] God everywhere" means "seeing God as Creator." That is not the best reading of the passage. The passage does not say that God is not *directly* present in nature, as Evans puts it. It simply says that "God is not there." That assertion is immediately followed by a contrasting kind of claim: "*but* within the individual there is a possibility" (emphasis mine). God is not in nature but a potentiality for a God-relationship is in the individual. When the potentiality for finding the God-relationship within oneself is realized, *then* one can "see God everywhere." That cannot mean that, then, one can see God in nature. After all, God is not there. So "seeing God everywhere" must mean something else.

On the page preceding the beginning of the passage, the omnipresence of God is contrasted with the omnipresence of a policeman. The contrast is that the policeman is visible and God is not. But certainly we are not to take the idea of the omnipresence of the policeman literally. Rather, the idea is one of being everywhere under obligation. Just as the ethical man, who "sees tasks everywhere," is not committed to nature's being infused with duty, one who "sees God everywhere" is not committed to a view of God in nature, even if God is thought of as invisible. Evans is right that the kind of move he speaks of here is attributed to Socrates in *Fragments*, and Socrates is praised for it. That praise is, however, not an endorsement of the move. Instead, the praise is by contrast to attempts to prove the existence of God from the facts of nature.

If, then, we are to attribute to Climacus the idea of God as Creator of nature, it should be on the basis of the language that is used in the passage that is in question, not on the basis of a movement of thought seen as suggested by the passage. We should be careful about making an attribution for that reason, though. Climacus is, after all, explicit about the fact that he is being critical of what he calls the "objective tendency." He is equally explicit about the fact that his approach involves the Socratic art—assuming the point of view to be criticized.

> By beginning straightway with ethical categories against the objective tendency, one does wrong and fails to hit the mark, because one has nothing in common with the attacked. But by remaining within the metaphysical, one can employ the comic, which also is in the metaphysical. (CUP 124)

Climacus's use of language that might suggest a view of God as a peculiar kind of metaphysical object ought not be seen, then, as a sign of Climacus's adoption of such a view.

When I say that the language in question *might suggest* a metaphysical view of God, I speak advisedly, because the language certainly does not *imply* such a view. God may be spoken of as Creator without assigning metaphysical status to ethical or religious concepts. Indeed, O. K. Bouwsma has argued that it is the imputation of metaphysical significance to the language of worship that led Anselm to the kind of argument that Climacus finds problematic.[13] That observation points to what Climacus probably had in mind by seeing the effort at proof as obstructive. Suppose that I address someone as "my dearest darling." It would be an utter absurdity to say that I presuppose that there exists and X such that X has darling-character and X has dearest-character. As long as one focusses on understanding some X characterized in a "dearest darling" way, nothing of a relationship in which that language is sensibly used occurs. As long I approach a person in such a posture as to insist that she reveal to me the ways in which she is dearest darling, I will never be moved to call her "my dearest darling."

The point is not that there is a singular object and clarity requires distinguishing one approach to that object from another approach to that same object. The point is that there are different kinds of enterprises and the approach one takes determines the kind of enterprise in which one is engaged. (King Lear's demand for proof of his daughters' love involved his failure to recognize that fact.) One way of seeing what is at issue here is to examine Climacus's claim that Christianity is "an existential communication."

Existence-Communication or Doctrine

Climacus tries to underscore the view that Christianity calls for essentially a personal relationship rather than an intellectual relationship to God by saying that "Christianity is not a doctrine* [Lære] but an existence-contradiction and an existence-communication" (CUP 379-80). As with the name/concept distinction, we need to ask here exactly what is being denied and what is being asserted. Climacus makes the distinction in order to avoid a misunderstanding, and he provided a footnote to explain the misunderstanding he hoped to avoid. Evans sees that effort as having inspired a misunderstanding, however, namely, the view that Christianity lacks "intellectual content."

---

[13]See "Anselm's Argument," in *Without Proof or Evidence: Essays of O. K. Bouwsma*, ed. J. L. Craft and R. E. Hustwit (Lincoln NB and London: University of Nebraska Press, 1984) 40-72.

Climacus gives an explanation of his point and an example of the kind of doctrine he is denying Christianity to be.

> If Christianity were a doctrine it would *eo ipso* not constitute the opposite to speculative thought, but would be an element within it. Christianity pertains to existence, to existing, but existence and existing are the very opposite of speculation. The Eleatic doctrine, for example, is not related to existing but to speculation; therefore it must be assigned its place within speculation. (CUP 380)

In the footnote, Climacus explains further. "Surely a philosophical theory that is to be comprehended and speculatively understood is one thing, and a doctrine that is to be actualized in existence is something else" (CUP 379n.). The explanation underscores an ambiguity in the term *Lære*, which may be translated as *doctrine* or as *teaching*. In the first instance, Climacus uses the term in a sense that entails having purely intellectual import. "[A] doctrine is not related to existing" (CUP 380). In the second instance, he uses the term in a sense that entails relevance to existing. Climacus is making clear that when he says that Christianity is not a "doctrine" (*Lære*), what he means is not that Christianity is not a "teaching" (*Lære*) at all, but that it is not a teaching that is a doctrine in that first sense. Evans points out that it would be a misunderstanding to read Climacus as denying that Christianity has "intellectual content." Climacus explicitly says that he is not saying that Christianity lacks "content." He does not provide the qualification of "content" as "intellectual." Just what it means to say that Christianity has intellectual content needs to be determined.

The qualification might be seen as functioning to save Climacus from an unintended redundance. After all, for something to be a teaching, it must be a teaching of something and cannot be "contentless." But Climacus does not need saving on that score, because precisely what he says is that it would be a deception to see his denial as implying that Christianity is contentless. "Furthermore, to say that Christianity is empty of content because it is not a doctrine is only chicanery" (CUP 380).

Perhaps the qualification serves to underscore that Climacus's denial of the purely intellectual import of Christianity does not entail a denial of *any* intellectual import. Determining what that would mean requires a closer look at Climacus's understanding of "doctrine/teaching." The example Climacus gives of the kind of doctrine that he denies Christianity to be is " 'everything is and nothing originates' (the Eleatics' doctrine)" (CUP 307). Climacus characterizes such a doctrine in two ways: (1) It is not related to existing. (2) It is a part of speculative thought. The latter characterization permits us to see Climacus as understanding "doctrine" in this sense to refer to a proposition or set of propositions understood as admitting of truth or falsity. So Climacus's denial that Christianity is a doctrine may be taken to mean that Christianity lacks at least one of the two characterizations mentioned, not necessarily that it lacks both. Evans's qualification of "content" may be taken to mean that what Climacus is saying is that Christianity is relevant to existing and so is not a doctrine in the first sense, but that Christianity contains propositions understood to be true and is, therefore, a doctrine in the second sense.

Indeed, Climacus may be seen as indirectly pointing to specific doctrinal contents of Christianity. He says, "If I were to say that Christianity is a doctrine about the Incarnation, about the Atonement, etc., misunderstanding would immediately be made easy" (CUP 381). This hypothetical form of locution is a device that Climacus uses to suggest something without asserting it. So, it might be inferred that Climacus does not assert that Christianity consists of certain doctrines believed to be true, not because he does not believe that it does, but because he wants to discourage focussing attention on that aspect of it.

We are in position now to see that the issues raised by the question of what it means to say that Christianity is not a doctrine but an existential communication are the same as those raised by the question of what it means to say that God is not a name but a concept. If, as I have claimed, to say that God is not a name but a concept is to say that speech in which that term is used is not a reference to some object about which some truth claim is being made, but the invocation of some regulative ideal, then the use of that term in Christianity is not the assertion of doctrines taken to be true but an appeal to a way of being/living. Evans's view is that according to Climacus, while the existential appeal is fundamental, both assertion and existential appeal are taking place. That amounts to a modification of the Climacian claim to have it say that God is not *primarily* a name, but a concept. Such a modification is unwarranted.

As was indicated, Climacus's indirect references to Christian "doctrine" may be taken to mean that he does see Christianity as having some content that is made up of assertions. It just happens that Christianity is not the sort of doctrine that "desires to be intellectually grasped," though it may be, on such a view. For such a view to be sustained, two obstacles must be overcome. (1) This way of reading Climacus is in clear conflict with the passage already cited, in which Climacus says that if Christianity were a doctrine it would not be the opposite of speculative thought. So Climacus is saying that Christianity is not a doctrine, not a part of speculative thought, not constituted by assertions. (2) It has to be shown that Climacus maintains that the content of Christianity is of a sort as to be capable of being intellectually grasped, not in the sense of *known* to be true but understood as having truth-value. For that to be done, the unmistakable impediment placed by Climacus must be overcome.

The impediment to viewing the content of Christianity as intellectually graspable in the above sense is Climacus's insistence on the paradoxical character of Christianity. As we have seen, the paradox that is the content of Christianity is an antinomous one. It has the form of a contradiction. The unknowable (named the Unknown) becomes known. For the sake of form, this may be expressed by saying that the unknowable is knowable or X is not-X. Something expressible in that form is simply not capable of being intellectually grasped, and so the challenge cannot include intellectually grasping it, even as a secondary consideration. The content of Christianity is expressible as a contradiction, if one operates from the Greek perspective, the perspective assumed by Johannes Climacus. So the challenge is to shed that perspective, a perspective that is characterized by a certain understanding of oneself.

The Eternal

In *Postscript*, the language in which the paradox is presented is somewhat different and Climacus comes closer to putting it explicitly in the form of a contradiction.

> [L]et us assume that the eternal, essential truth itself is the paradox. How does the paradox emerge? By placing the eternal, essential truth together with existing. Consequently, if we place

> it together in the truth itself, the truth becomes a paradox. The eternal truth has come into existence in time. That is the paradox. (CUP 209)

> What then is the absurd? The absurd is that the eternal truth has come into existence in time, that God has come into existence, has been born, has grown up, etc., has come into existence exactly like any other individual human being, quite indistinguishable from any other human being. (CUP 210)

Two points in particular need attention. (1) The constitution of the paradox requires that "eternal" be understood as entailing being outside time. (2) The expression "the eternal truth" is used interchangeably with "God."

(1) To say that "X has come into being in time" is paradoxical implies that X is not such as to be capable of coming into being in time, that X is essentially outside time. The term "eternal" is generally thought to have precisely that significance. So while Climacus stops short of explicitly articulating the paradox in the form of a contradiction, there is a very short step from what he says to that explicit form.

(2) It is, also, generally thought that if anything is a fit subject for qualification by the term "eternal," it is God. We need to be more precise than consideration of what is generally thought, however. The concept of the "eternal" as timeless and as applicable to God is present in Greek philosophical thought. Parmenides makes the case for Being as changeless, timeless, and unitary. The attributes mentioned become the predicates of perfection that are the marks of Being in the primary sense, the Good, in Plato. In Aristotle, this is God. "[T]here necessarily is eternal changeless primary being" (*Metaphysics* 1071 b 3-4). "There must . . . be a principle such that its very nature is to be in act" (*Metaphysics* 1071 b 20). "[T]he activity of mind is also its life, and the divine is that activity. The self-sufficient activity of the divine is life at its eternal best. We maintain, therefore, that the divine is the eternal best living being, so that the divine is life unending, continuous, and eternal" (*Metaphysics* 1072 b 28-30). Involvement in time would be an imperfection, since change is an imperfection, whatever its source. If change were due to *physis*, internal nature, it would mean that the thing had not realized itself. If it were due to *dynamis*, the potentiality for being affected by something else, it

would mean that the thing was not self-sufficient. Consequently, God is the Unmoved Mover, having itself as its object—"a divine mind knows itself" (*Metaphysics* 1074 b 33)—and moving other things only by being the object of love (*Metaphysics* 1072b 1-4).

Just as in *Fragments*, (by using the term the Unknown) the Greek conception of God is invoked in constituting the Absolute Paradox, in *Postscript*, the Greek conception of God as eternal is used in constituting the paradox. Given the Greek view of God as timeless, the paradox becomes an antinomous one, formulatable as a contradiction. That does not present an intellectual challenge, but an intellectual impossibility. The challenge is to convert the antinomy into what looks like a veridical paradox. That conversion would be a conversion of oneself, however, a conversion in which the Greek ideal of perfection is discarded. The point here should not be misunderstood. It is not about changing an intellectual position. It is about changing oneself in a fundamental way—from seeing the ideal in intellectual terms to seeing the ideal in ethical terms. To paraphrase the young Kierkegaard, it is from seeing oneself in terms of what one is to know to seeing oneself in terms of what one is to do.

So far so good, it might be said, but that is not far enough. The conversion is not to what just looks like a veridical paradox but to what is a veridical paradox. Once the change in oneself has taken place, then one is in position to see the truth of the Christian claim. Heightened subjectivity is necessary for appreciation of the truth. As Climacus puts it, "truth is subjectivity." Before the question of what that means is addressed, some other considerations need to be made. The significance of the interchangeable use of "God" and "Truth" needs to be considered by exploring one other aspect of Climacus's understanding of the concept of God and Climacus's understanding of the concept of truth. These explorations will show that Climacus understands God as the ideal of self, as already argued, that truth is used synonymously with God, and that since subjectivity is used to mean selfhood, "Truth is subjectivity." is tautologous.

One avenue to an understanding of the concept of God operating in the Climacian writings proceeds through the discussion of offense in *Fragments* and Kierkegaard's remark in connection with *Fragments* about "Feuerbach's indirect service to Christianity as the offended individual . . . " (P V B 9). Climacus recognizes two possible responses to the Absolute Paradox, faith and offense.

> If the paradox and the understanding meet in the mutual understanding of their difference, then the encounter is a happy one. . . . If the encounter is not in mutual understanding, then the relation is unhappy, and the understanding's unhappy love . . . which . . . resembles only the unhappy love rooted in misunderstood self-love . . . we could more specifically call offense. (PF 49)

Offense, then, is the self-assertiveness of the understanding in the face of the paradox as distinct from the "step[ping] aside" which is called faith (PF 59).

A form in which this self-assertiveness may be manifested, according to Climacus, is the phenomenon he calls "an acoustical illusion."

> When the understanding cannot get the paradox into its head, this did not have its origin in the understanding but in the paradox itself, which was paradoxical enough to have the effrontery to call the understanding a clod and a dunce who at best can say "yes" and "no" to the same thing, which is not good theology. So it is with offense. Everything it says about the paradox it has learned from the paradox, even though, making use of an acoustical illusion, it insists that it itself has originated the paradox. (PF 53)

So, in offense, the understanding echoes the paradox, but mistakenly attributes to itself what the paradox says.

Let us note, now, what Feuerbach says that can be seen as the manifestation of his offense. What Marx did in applying the Hegelian concept of alienation in the sphere of politics, Feuerbach did in the sphere of religion. According to Marx, perfections that rightly belong to persons are attributed to the State. For example, human equality, that is, indifference to social status and other distinctions, is a mark of the State, while in actual social intercourse, social status is of enormous importance. In political life, man is thus separated from his ideal self. According to Feuerbach, religion has its basis in man's essence, in that which essentially distinguishes man from animal, namely, self-consciousness. That distinguishing mark is an early form of self-knowledge. As such, it is consciousness of man as he is potentially—infinite, perfect, eternal, almighty, and holy. In religion, however, these qualities are attributed to an external object, God, and man is seen as having the contrary qualities—finitude, imperfection, temporality, weakness, and sinfulness. Religion, thus, creates a gulf between man and his essential self and that is alienation—the estrangement of man from himself. The view of man in religion is in error, Feuerbach says, for "every being is in and by itself infinite—has its God, its highest conceivable being, in itself."[14] Accordingly, he writes:

> The truth is only the identity of God and man. Religion is truth only when it affirms human attributes as divine, falsehood when in the form of theology, it denies these attributes, separating God from man as a different being. (333)

Feuerbach's qualification as the offended individual is not due to any denial of what the Paradox says but his assumption of credit for it. He thinks himself to have arrived at the idea of the identity of God and man from a rational analysis of the phenomenon of religion. That identity, however, is the specific claim of Christianity. Feuerbach's claim exemplifies the "acoustical illusion," since he attributes the claim of the paradox to Reason. But by making the claim that he does, Feuerbach undermines the notion of God as majestically otherworldly and that is, no doubt, the indirect service to Christianity that Kierkegaard had in mind. That assessment of Feuerbach contrasts with the scorn expressed for the self-importance assumed by orthodoxy in defending Christianity against the likes of Feuerbach by making it "the most elevated and the most profound and the one and only thing that can lend true luster to this life . . . " (P VIII-1 A 434).

Climacus is, then, in agreement with Feuerbach about the status of the concept of God. He does not agree about its source or about the appropriate content, but about its status as the regulative ideal of humanity that is within the person. This is not just Climacus's view of. It is a view that is shared by the pseudonym Anti-Climacus, who represents one who is a Christian to an extraordinary degree, in contrast to Climacus, who says he is not a Christian. Anti-Climacus writes:

---

[14]Ludwig Feuerbach, *The Essence of Christianity*, trans. George Eliot (New York, Evanston, London: Harper & Row, 1957) 7.

No, the earlier dogmatic was right in asserting that the fact that sin was against God infinitely potentiated it. Their fault lay in regarding God as something external, and in assuming that it was only now and then that one sinned against God. But God is not something external in the sense that a policeman is. What must be understood is that the self has the conception (*Forestillingen*) of God. (SUD 211)

Like Climacus, Anti-Climacus uses "God" and "the conception of God" interchangeably. Understanding that avoids the trivialization of Climacus's remark that would read him as saying that the conception of God, as distinct from the referent of the conception, is in the self.

It might be objected, however, that all this does is to make Climacus and Anti-Climacus guilty of similar incoherence. After all, Climacus says that "the believer . . . is different from an ethicist by being infinitely interested in the actuality of another . . . " (CUP 324). He also says that Religiousness B or Christianity involves a "break with immanence" (CUP 571). Along the same lines, Anti-Climacus speaks of the self as a "derived, constituted . . . relation . . . a relation which relates itself to its own self, and in relating itself to its own self relates itself to another" (SUD 146), this other being the power that constituted it. Since that is what the self is, a healthy self is one that "by relating itself to its own self and by willing to be itself the self is grounded transparently in the Power which posited it" (*Sickness* 147). That Power is, of course, God. Thus, both Climacus and Anti-Climacus might be seen as making inconsistent claims, and a case needs to be made for accepting one set of claims rather than the other as genuinely theirs.

First, with respect to Anti-Climacus's view, it is important to notice what he does and does not say. Note that he does not say that the self is a relation that by relating itself to another relates itself to itself. Rather, he says that by relating itself to itself, it relates itself to another. He, also, does not say that by being grounded in the power that posited it, the self relates itself to itself. Rather, he says that by relating itself to itself, the self is grounded in the power that posited it. This is to say that being grounded in the constituting power is not something essentially distinct from the self's relating itself to itself. There is, then, no need to suppose that the constituting power is external to the self. This may become clearer when seen in light of Climacus's view.

Climacus explicitly speaks of Christianity as the religion of transcendence, as involving a break with immanence. It would be a mistake to simply translate Climacus's speaking about transcendence into talk about otherworldliness. Understanding what Climacus means by calling Christianity the religion of transcendence requires understanding in relation to what he sees Christianity as transcendent, that is, what he understands by "immanence." The religion of immanence, "Religiousness A is the dialectic of inward deepening; it is the relation to an eternal happiness that is not conditioned by a something . . . " (CUP 556). "Religiousness A can be present in paganism . . . " (CUP 557). Indeed, that is what is represented by Socrates in *Fragments*. The contrasts drawn between Religiousness A and B are precisely the ones drawn between the Socratic and the alternative paradoxical view. Indeed, Climacus makes explicit the fact that he is elaborating on remarks made in *Fragments*. (See esp. CUP 573n.)

Now, the Socratic view is one in which the highest possibility for a person is built in by nature and, through "recollection," through thinking, one can attain to an understanding of one's essential self and, by virtue of that, become one's essential self. That is the view that rationality is the defining feature of self. On the generalized version of that view, whatever happens flows out of what preceded it in accordance with laws that are accessible by thought. That is why Climacus sees Religiousness A as allied with speculative thought without identifying it with speculative thought. "Religiousness A . . . is not speculation but nonetheless is speculative . . . " (CUP 570). It is this view in relation to which Climacus sees Christianity as transcendent. Thus, the break with immanence is expressible as "a break with all thinking" (CUP 579). Transcendence, then, means beyond that view of self and world represented by Socrates and a philosophy that presumes to capture everything in a systematic whole.

When Climacus says, then, that "Christianity will not be content to be an evolution within the total category of human nature" (CUP 559), he is to be understood as saying that with the entrance of Christianity, a radically new possibility for a person comes into being. This is to say that Christianity is not the outgrowth of some prior point of development in accordance with laws of nature and of thought. The fundamental assumption of immanence is discarded. What God is (what the self is) is not worked out by thought. God is, rather, presented as embodied. God appears as a particular human being. "[I]n the paradoxical-religious, the eternal is present at a specific point, and this is the break with immanence" (CUP 571).

It is clear, then, that in the paradoxical religion, God is not eternally latent in the individual. Rather, "the individual relates himself to something outside himself" (CUP 561). Note, however, that Climacus is speaking of the initial situation, for a transformation must have taken place for one to have become a believer. Climacus puts it this way:

> The existing person must have lost continuity with himself, must have become someone else (not different from himself within himself), and now, by receiving the condition from the god, becomes a new creation. The contradiction is that becoming a Christian begins with the miracle of creation. (CUP 576)

What takes place, then, is the imparting to the individual of what was eternally latent in the individual according to Religiousness A. The individual now has the condition for the Truth within him. An attempt to explain the later state of the individual would involve making an appeal to an earlier state of the individual and showing how that earlier state contained some potentiality, such that the circumstances being propitious, the later state occurred. But that is precisely what Christianity claims cannot be done. That is what makes for the break with immanence. That is what would make the later state a genuine creation. That is what would make its occurrence inexplicable, that is, a miracle. (The explanation I have offered of how the Absolute Paradox is constituted is not, then, in conflict with Climacus's insistence that the Paradox cannot be understood.)

Once the transition has been made to a view of God as made present at a definite time, God is appropriated and is no longer external. In *Fragments*, Climacus puts it this way:

> Faith is itself a [miracle] (*Under*), and everything that is true of the paradox is also of faith. But within this [miracle] everything is again [Socratic]. (PF 65)

Everything is again Socratic in the sense that God is now in the person. God implants himself.

> When an oak nut is planted in a clay pot, the pot breaks; when new wine is poured into old leather bottles, they burst. What happens, then, when the god plants himself in the frailty of a human being if he does not become a new person and a new vessel! (PF 34)

In the Climacian view, then, God is in the self and the apparent inconsistency between that position and other remarks made by Climacus is due to differences in perspective, specifically, to whether one is speaking about God and self before or after God has been appropriated.

If Climacus is saved from inconsistency, is it not at the expense of convicting him of triviality? After all, if God is the defining feature of self, that is, if God is that which makes a self to be a self, is it not tautologically true to say that God is in the self? Climacus would, no doubt, plead guilty to the charge of tautology but not of triviality. A tautology is not trivial if what it asserts has been obscured. As Ralph Johnson pointed out, an important part of Kierkegaard's task was to combat forgetfulness.[15] Sometimes it takes a tautology to do that.[16] A tautology is not trivial if the prevailing view opposes it. Feuerbach's attempt to undermine religion by locating divine attributes in man illustrates the prevalence of the view in religion that God is something external. His recogni-

---

[15]Ralph Johnson, *The Concept of Existence in Concluding Unscientific Postscript* (The Hague: Martinus Nijhoff, 1972) 173-209.

[16]Laszlo Versenyi argues that Protagoras's statement that man is the measure of all things is a tautology. (He says "nearly tautological." He points out that the term Protagoras used that is translated as "things" is *chremata*. "Protagoras's use of *chremata*—rather than *onta* or even *pragmata*—becomes exceedingly appropriate, for the original meaning of *chremata* is not just things, beings, or objects in general, but things with a special relation to our involvement with them: things one uses or needs; goods, property, etc.; generalized into affairs, events, matters we are concerned with." ("Protagoras's Man-Measure Fragment," *American Journal of Philology* 83 (1962): 182.) And Versenyi goes on to point out that the statement is not trivial in a context in which Parmenidean assumptions about the object of thought prevail.

tion that God is in man is his indirect service to Christianity. On that point, he is in agreement with Climacus.

Faith, Truth, and Subjectivity

Since, in Climacus's view, God is not some peculiar object of knowledge, faith, understood as the appropriate relationship to God, is not some peculiar cognitive stance in which that relationship is attained. Maintaining that Climacus does not see God as some object of knowledge, then, requires arguing against the view that Climacus sees faith as constitutive of knowledge in some way. The view in question is one that is shared by defenders and detractors of Kierkegaard. The focus of that view is the well-known dictum in *Postscript* that truth is subjectivity. What is shared by the two sides is the attribution to Climacus of an argument. What is not shared is the assessment of that argument. The argument might be represented as follows:

(1) Faith involves an act of will.
(2) Will is subjective.
(3) Faith is required for truth.
(4) Truth is subjective.

This argument seems to be the kernel of positions taken in attacks on and defenses of Kierkegaard. The first premise is clearly ascribable to Climacus. The second premise is uncontroversial. Even if one adopted a deterministic stance, one would still hold that the object of the will is partly determined by the makeup of the individual and that being an object of will does not imply being an object in fact. Since, the conclusion is taken to be, on the one hand, ludicrous or, at best, mistaken, or, on the other hand, insightful and true, the matter tends to turn on the meaning of and the basis for the third premise. The positions taken see the argument as a gambit in a defense of Christianity.

There is no question that there is argumentation that takes place in the Climacian writings. Understanding the writings, then, requires assessing the arguments. Assessing the arguments as formal structures, however, is not sufficient for understanding the writings. We saw that to be the case with arguments in *Meno*. There Socrates made two arguments with conflicting conclusions about whether or not virtue can be taught. If we are only attentive to the assessment of the arguments as formal arguments and have no regard for the overall job being done by them with respect to the other parties in the dialogue and the expected audience, we will simply fail to understand the work.

With that in mind, we should be skeptical about what we have gotten from someone who says in his conclusion, as Pojman does,

> I have tried to show that Kierkegaard can be examined as a philosopher who sets forth theses and defends them, who uses reason to establish his theses. I have examined their content as well as his arguments, especially those in the published Climacus writings.[17]

That may sound like nobility of philosophical purpose, "the lofty equanimity of the scholar," but it means that the texts were mined for argument without consideration of "indirect communication." In fact, in an earlier version of the particular arguments in question, Pojman says this about his task:

> The main lines of the argument in the *Concluding Unscientific Postscript* are diffuse, devious and difficult to state precisely. This is no doubt due to the fact that Kierkegaard is concerned to communicate indirectly. What follows is an attempt to make explicit what Climacus makes implicit: the central propositions and inferences involved in an argument in defence of Christian faith.[18]

Thus, indirect communication seems to be regarded as an obstacle to be overcome in clear philosophical exposition and examination of argument. As is appropriate for that assessment, it is treated in an appendix in Pojman's book.

If Climacus was engaged in a defense of Christianity, then he would have been guilty of a tremendous stupidity, in the eyes of Anti-Climacus, who remarked on "how extraordinarily stupid it is to defend Christianity . . . " (SUD 218). Assuming that a defense in the form of argument is what constitutes a "learned defense," he would be guilty disfiguring Christianity, in the eyes of Kierke-

---

[17]Louis Pojman, *The Logic of Subjectivity* (University AL: University of Alabama Press, 1984) 144.

[18]Louis Pojman, "Kierkegaard on Justification of Belief," *International Journal for Philosophy of Religion* 8/2 (1977): 78.

gaard.[19] Since Pojman minimizes the differences between the pseudonyms and Kierkegaard, he might well have asked why Climacus would be inclined to do what is seen as stupid and distortive by Anti-Climacus and Kierkegaard.

While there is no mention of truth as subjectivity in *Fragments*, the positions articulated by the first and third premises in the argument attributed to Climacus are unmistakably there. So, given the uncontroversial nature of the second premise, it might not seem unreasonable to ascribe the argument to *Fragments*. As I have shown earlier, however, the concept of truth employed in *Fragments* is not the concept that plays a role in epistemological theories. Hence, the view that the argument is a ploy in the defense of Christianity on some kind of epistemological grounds is mistaken.

Three facts would seem to invite that view, however, and they need to be considered. (1) There is ostensibly an argument in the first chapter of *Fragments*, one that I have presented, that has as one of its conclusion the claim that willing is a necessary condition for acquiring the truth. (2) There is clear invocation of epistemological considerations in the explanation of the concept of faith in the chapter called "Interlude" in *Fragments*. (3) There is ostensibly a critique of the classical formula for truth as a lead-in to the statement that truth is subjectivity in *Postscript*.

I have shown that the "argument" presenting the un-Socratic alternative is a pretense on Climacus's part. It is a conscious effort to appear to spin the fabric of Christianity out of pure thought. Even if we were to suppose that it did represent a serious argument, close inspection would expose a serious shortcoming on the very point of concern here. There is absolutely nothing said argumentatively on behalf of the claim that willing is a necessary condition for acquiring the truth. That omission stands in stark contrast to and is set in relief by a clear argument for the insufficiency of willing.[20]

---

[19]Søren Kierkegaard, *Works of Love*, trans. Howard Hong and Edna Hong (New York: Harper & Brothers, 1962) 193.

[20]The following argument for the thesis about the relationship between willing and acquiring the truth is presented in Benjamin Daise "The Will to Truth in Kierkegaard's Philosophical Fragments," *Philosophy of Religion* (January 1992).

The insufficiency of willing is established by a *reductio* argument. Suppose, Climacus says, that the learner were by his will alone able to set himself free, to acquire the truth by himself. If so, he would have had in himself the condition that is essential for attaining the truth. That, however, is consistent with the Socratic perspective and inconsistent with the hypothesis negating that perspective. "According to the hypothesis, then, he will not be able to set himself free" (PF 17).

The argument above is made immediately after the introduction of the idea that willing is necessary. "But first of all, he must will it" (PF 16). The effect of this presentation and immediate move to argument for another point is that this point is not argued at all. Indeed, it could be argued that on the basis of Climacus's hypothesis, there is no necessity of willing. If the learner did not have the truth and the teacher brings it to him, the moment would still be of decisive significance even if the teacher imposed the truth upon the learner. Such an imposition would certainly not return us to the Socratic, which supposes that the learner already had the truth.

The shortcoming in the argument amounts to exposure of the need for importing assumptions in order to make the picture that is supposedly sketched on the basis of the hypothesis conform to the Christian story. That conformity is achieved simply by importing the assumptions from the story to which the sketch is to conform. The necessity of willing is derived from consideration of the specific object of the will as it is understood in the Christian story. That is to say, it is because of what Christianity specifically regards as the truth that willing to have the truth is a necessary condition for acquiring it.

The general conception of truth operating in *Fragments* is that it is an idea of self, an understanding of what it is to realize oneself as a person. Nothing about that general idea implies the necessity of willing. Indeed, in *Either/Or* II, Judge Wilhelm exhorts the young man of the first volume to break with the natural stance by choosing himself. According to the judge, by living a life devoted to the pursuit of pleasure and the avoidance of displeasure, the young man is not living a life of his choosing. He has not willed the idea that governs him. He is what he is "by nature," as it were, not by choice.

The alternative offered by the judge may be subject to analysis leading to the same conclusion. That analysis, which would involve close inspection of both volumes of *Either/Or*, can only be suggested here. It involves recognition that in Volume I, there is an understanding of self as essentially a solitary, atomistic individual, whose well-being is antagonistic to the well-being of others. That view of self is expressed in the counsel offered up in "Rotation of Crops." Avoid marriage, friendship, and official position. (EOI 295-98)

That view of self is the same as that held by the Sophist Antiphon and is captured by his understanding of justice. "Justice then consists in not transgressing the customs of the city in which one enjoys citizenship. So a man would employ justice best for his own interests if he were to regard the laws as important when witnesses were present, but, when no witnesses are present, he were to regard the demands of nature as important. For the demands of the laws are artificial, but the demands of nature are necessary."[21] This is the view presented by Glaucon in book 2 of *Republic* as the challenge to Socrates. There the city is seen as arising out of a contract, the aim of which is to avoid being harmed with impunity but at the expense of forgoing attempting to harm others with impunity. Civil society is seen as unnatural. It conflicts with "the desire for undue gain which every creature by nature pursues as good" (*Republic* 359c).

The basis of the alternative view that is developed into the picture of the ideal polis is that each person is essentially a part of a community, not essentially an atomic and discrete entity. "I think that a city comes to be, . . . " Socrates responds, "because not one of us is self-sufficient, but needs many things" (*Republic* 369b). Ethical requirements, on this view, are the natural and rational developments of this view of self.

Broadly speaking, this is the ethical idea of self operating in the Kierkegaardian corpus. There are identifiably Kantian and Hegelian features, but despite the differences in details in the Kantian and Hegelian views, they share the general idea of the

---

[21]*The Older Sophists*, ed. Rosamond Kent Sprague (Columbia: University of South Carolina Press, 1972) 218-19.

ethical self as essentially a part of a larger whole. While Kant immediately understands that larger whole as the class of rational beings, Hegel sees a development from the family, to civil society, to the State. The portrayal of the ethical man in *Either/Or* II as a married man and father (family man) and as a judge (civil servant) is a figurative way of capturing the ethical idea of self.

The picture of the ethical self presented is, of course, an idealized one and it makes no mention of the tensions felt by a person who understands himself ethically. Those tensions involve precisely the pulls of the demands by different larger groups that make a claim on one's loyalty, on one's understanding of oneself. Those tensions are recognized in the account of the tragic hero in *Fear and Trembling*. Agamemnon's paternal duty to his daughter, who must be sacrificed to appease the gods and permit the ships to sail towards Troy on the mission of the State is in tension with the duty that demands pursuit of the mission. (Interestingly, it was fraternal duty to Agamemnon's brother, whose wife, Helen, had been taken, that gave rise to the commitment of the resources of the State in the first place.) So, the view of the ethical idea in the works acknowledge ethical struggle, but that struggle is seen as one aimed at finding the expression of the appropriate whole of which one is a part.

Now, the demands of the societal whole are manifested in a variety of institutions and institutional rules. Those are the inherited results of rational efforts to order our lives in such a way as to achieve the greatest good. As the conditions of life are not static, there is also ethical struggle to adjust institutions and rules to meet the challenges of new conditions. Questions regarding a right to die and affirmative action, for example, require rethinking rules in light of conditions that are relatively new. Whether one identifies oneself with the traditional rules or with the demand for new rules, the same kind of fundamental understanding of self is involved.

Societal expectations are also informal. Even where no formal rules govern, your language, your job, your physical appearance, your place of residence make a difference to how you are judged as a person. Those considerations, then, enter into our understanding of what it takes to be the kind of person we ought to be.

Since we are socialized into those formal and informal expectations, they belong to us, as it were, "by nature." It is by societal nature, to be sure, but the point is that it is our environment that thrusts them on us or inculcates them in us, and no act of will is needed to identify ourselves with them. The specific content of the idea of self, of truth as it is understood in the un-Socratic alternative, requires breaking with what one is given, as we saw earlier. It is for that reason that willing is seen as a necessary condition for attaining truth. Nothing in the so-called hypothesis yields that requirement. There is no argument for it. It is not part of an argument in defense of Christianity. It is not part of an argument in the construction of Christianity. It is simply drawn from Christianity. As Kierkegaard wrote, "To act as if Christianity were the invention of Johannes Climacus is precisely the biting satire on philosophy's impudence towards it" (P VI A 84).

The object of will, then, in *Fragments* is noncognitive. The object is an ideal of self, and the act of willing is acceptance of that ideal as appropriately governing one's life. This is a view that is held by Kierkegaard throughout his authorship. As early as 1834, he wrote, "Faith certainly requires an expression of will, and yet *in another sense* than when, for example, I must say that all cognition requires an expression of will . . . " (P I A 36; emphasis mine). As late as 1854 or 1855, he wrote, "In the New Testament faith is presented as having not an intellectual but an ethical character; it signifies the relationship of personality between God and man" (P XI-2 A 380). Given that alone, it would be surprising that the concept of faith in *Fragments* came to be seen as dependent on Kierkegaard's epistemology. The reason that this happened concerns the second fact that needs to be addressed, namely the appeal to epistemological concepts in "Interlude." The important question is: What is the role of the epistemological considerations made?

One way of viewing the relationship between Kierkegaard's epistemology and his concept of faith is to see Kierkegaard as making the Kantian move of denying knowledge in order to make room for faith. On that view, Kierkegaard is seen as holding an epistemological theory that results in skepticism and which leaves one no choice but to rely on belief with respect to ordinary empirical matters. Since belief is seen as containing a subjective component, faith becomes no less epistemologically respectable for having a subjective component.

There are several variations on this idea. In Popkin's "Kierkegaard and Skepticism,"[22] the idea is put forth in language that is close to the language I have just used. That idea is also the germ of the argument put forth by Paul Edwards in his account of the failure of Kierkegaard's attempt to justify Christianity by claiming that truth is subjective. Edwards sees that claim as an attempt to deny singular legitimacy to any knowledge claim, thereby paving the way to legitimacy of the claim of Christianity.[23] In each case, the epistemological theory is seen as providing the foundation for the legitimacy of faith as it is understood by Kierkegaard. Even someone as different from Popkin and Edwards as Evans sees a relationship of dependence between a Kierkegaardian epistemology and Kierkegaard's view of faith. Evans argues that the inadequacy of foundationalism as an epistemological theory shows the need for inclusion of a subjective component in any justification of knowledge claims.[24] Consequently, what is essential in faith, according to Evans, far from being at variance with what an adequate account of knowledge must include, is in fact essential to such an account.

It cannot be denied that most of "Interlude" is devoted to developing a view in which certainty is denied to all but statements that are reports either of "immediate sensation" or "immediate cognition." Whether such a view is labelled foundationalism, justificationism, or something else is unimportant. It is equally unimportant whether Climacus means by "immediate sensation" something captured by ordinary locutions such as "seeing" or "hearing" or if he means something like "sense data," "the given," "data simpliciter," etc. The point that he wants to make is that all historical judgments and, in particular, all judgments about coming

---

[22]Richard Popkin, "Kierkegaard and Skepticism," *Kierkegaard: A Collection of Critical Essays*, ed. Josiah Thompson (Garden City NY: Doubleday, 1972) 368.

[23]Paul Edwards, "Kierkegaard and the Truth of Christianity," *Philosophy* 46/176 (April 1971): 93.

[24]C. Stephen Evans, "Kierkegaard and Plantinga on Belief in God: Subjectivity as the Ground of Properly Basic Religious Beliefs," *Faith and Philosophy* 5/1 (January 1988): 31.

into existence fall outside the scope of what can be known with certainty, because they are judgments about what is not available to immediate sensation or immediate cognition, however those may be understood. Consequently, according to Climacus, all historical judgments involve an act of will, a decision to accept something as being true without adequate justification or at least without the kind of justification that is required for certainty. Judgments of that kind are called beliefs. To put it another way, historical events are the objects of belief, not knowledge.

What was the point of Climacus's epistemological excursion? The point is articulated in two pages at the end of "Interlude," two pages labelled "Appendix"—"Application." Climacus is rather straightforward about his understanding of the application. According to him, what has been said applies to ordinary historical events. But it also applies to the extraordinary historical event that is the subject of the un-Socratic alternative presented earlier, with one essential difference.

> What has been said here applies to the . . . [ordinary] (*ligefrem*) historical, whose contradiction is only that it has come into existence. . . .
> We shall now return to our poem and to our assumption that the god has been. With respect to the ordinary historical, it holds true that it cannot become historical for immediate sensation or cognition. . . . But that historical fact (the content of our poem) has a unique quality in that it is not . . . [an ordinary] historical fact but a fact based upon a self-contradiction. . . . Yet it is a historical fact, and only for faith. (PF 86-87)[25]

The relationship represented in that account is clearly an analogous one. There is an analogy constructed between belief, ordinarily understood, and faith. The epistemological excursion develops one side of the analogy. It says how belief is to be understood. The last two pages of "Interlude" say that faith is like belief in some way and radically different in another way. It involves willing, but it

---

[25]I follow Swenson in rendering *ligefrem* as "ordinary" rather than as "direct," as Hong does. What is being talked about is referred to as wondrous or miraculous—out of the ordinary. So the distinction involved is understandable as one between an ordinary and an extraordinary fact. I cannot make sense of a direct/indirect fact distinction.

involves willing "in another sense." Insofar as the epistemological view developed is constructed for the sake of the analogy, for throwing light on faith, its adequacy or inadequacy is irrelevant to the account of faith. Arguing about whether or not the view is adequate is like arguing about whether or not a hand that is being used to point to a target has the right number of fingers. What is said in that debate might be of interest to the anatomist but the speaker would show himself to be out of the hunt.

What, though, is the analogy and the point of its breakdown as an analogy? The analogy is that just as in the case of ordinary historical events, the god's coming into existence is historical and cannot be apprehended with certainty. There is less than conclusive evidence in the ordinary case as well as in this case. The analogy breaks down, however, insofar as while the ordinary case may admit of degrees of confirmation, of varying weights of evidence for and against, the case of the god's coming into existence admits of no evidence one way or the other. Indeed, considered purely intellectually, it is an impossibility. It is "based upon a self-contradiction" (PF 88). So, the analogy is that ordinary belief and faith involve the absence of complete confirmation. The disanalogy is that the idea of confirmation, while conceivable with respect to the object of belief, is inconceivable with respect to the object of faith.

Thus, we see that the appeal to epistemological considerations in "Interlude" is not made in order to serve as a basis for claiming the truth of Christianity. Indeed, Climacus says, "It is not a question here of the truth of it but of assenting to the god's having come into existence . . . " (PF 87). There is clearly no reason, then, to see Climacus as attempting to support a truth claim when he says explicitly that truth, as opposed to falsity, is not at issue.

The third factual basis for seeing Climacus as engaged in a defense of Christianity is the fact that there is apparently a critique of the classical formula for truth that is a prelude to his statement that truth is subjectivity. If Climacus is not engaged in the same kind of enterprise as the proponents of the understanding of truth in that formula, why should he bother with it in the first place? Actually, we have already seen the general answer given by Climacus—that it is a mistake to begin immediately with ethical categories in the critique of the objective tendency. We need to look specifically as what is done in this case, however.

According to the classical formula, truth consists in the agreement of thought and its object. Wittgenstein's *Tractatus* captures the heart of that view in the following propositions:

4   A thought is a proposition with a sense.
4.2   The sense of a proposition is its agreement and disagreement with possibilities of existence and nonexistence of states of affairs.
4.21   The simplest kind of proposition, an elementary proposition, asserts the existence of a state of affairs.
4.25   If an elementary proposition is true, the state of affairs exists: if an elementary proposition is false, the state of affairs does not exist.
4.26   If all true elementary propositions are given, the result is a complete description of the world. (*Tractatus*)

Now, if we add to the above, the fact that any individual engaged in the pursuit of truth has limitations that make it impossible to gather all true propositions, elementary or not, we could (1) adjust the notion of truth to include that fact or (2) regard truth as something aimed at but not attainable. The two options are expressible as follows:

Truth is a character which attaches to an abstract proposition, such as a person might utter. It essentially depends upon that proposition's not professing to be exactly true. . . . Truth is that concordance of an abstract statement with the ideal limit towards which endless investigation would tend to bring scientific belief, which concordance the abstract statement may possess by virtue of the confession of its inaccuracy and one sidedness, and this confession is an essential ingredient of truth.[26]

The passage above does not come from Kierkegaard, but from Charles Sanders Peirce. It includes considerations on the basis of which one could say that when the object of thought "is understood as empirical being, truth itself is transformed into a *desideratum* [something wanted] and everything is placed in the process of becoming [*Vorden*], because the empirical object is not finished and

---

[26]Charles Sanders Peirce, *Collected Papers*, vols. 5-6, ed. Charles Hartshorne and P. Weiss (Cambridge MA: Harvard University Press, 1965) 394-95.

the existing knowing spirit is itself in process of becoming . . . "
(CUP 189). That is by Climacus. It also includes considerations on
the basis of which one could say that insofar as thought, an
essential ingredient of truth, is conditioned by perspective, truth
itself is so conditioned and is, to that extent, subjective. This
statement is not made by Climacus.

What Climacus *does* say is that truth is subjectiv-*ity* (CUP 181,
203, 204, 207). The significance of noting the form of the word is
that it indicates that the "is" in Climacus's remark about truth,
functions as the "is" of identity rather than as the copula used in
attribution. It says *what* truth is, not *what kind* of thing truth is. It
tells us that truth is constituted by subjectivity, not by the
thought/object relationship.

Just what does Climacus mean by saying that, and why would
he say it? A close look at the text reveals that as Climacus uses the
terms, saying that truth is subjectivity is tautologous and the
tautology functions as we saw tautology functioning before for
Climacus—to remind. It is easy to understand "subjectivity" as
referring to the idiosyncratic and the egoistic. When that is the
case, the "truth is subjectivity" dictum becomes radical individual
relativism. Climacus explicitly disavows that understanding for
precisely the reasons his critics do. Concerning the advice one
might be given to "divest himself of his subjectivity," he writes:

> [I]t is easy to see what this guidance understands by being a so-
> called subject of sorts, that it thereby quite correctly understands
> the accidental, the angular, the selfish, the eccentric, etc., of which
> every human being can have plenty. Christianity does not deny,
> either, that such things are to be discarded; . . . But the difference
> is simply that science and scholarship want to teach that becom-
> ing objective is the way, whereas Christianity teaches that the
> way is to become subjective; *that is truly to become a subject.* (CUP
> 131; my emphasis)

Note that there is a negatively expressed goal that Climacus sees
Christianity as sharing with those who now criticize him for anti-
intellectualism and irresponsibility. That goal is divestiture of
subjectivity. The disagreement arises about how that is to be done.
Climacus's prescription (on behalf of Christianity) is to become
subjective. That paradox (Get rid of subjectivity by becoming
subjective.) should alert us to the fact that attention needs to be

paid to he meaning of "subjectivity." The term is clearly being used equivocally. (This is reminiscent of Judge Wilhelm's counsel for getting rid of despair. "But if you do not want to be a poet, then there is no other way for you [to overcome despair] than the one I have pointed out to you: Despair!" [EOII 211].)

Before presenting the advice to become subjective, Climacus had already indicated how he and Christianity understand "subjectivity."

> Christianity wants to give the single individual an eternal happiness, a good that is not distributed in bulk but only to one, and to one at a time. Even though Christianity assumes that subjectivity, as the possibility of appropriation, is the possibility of receiving this good, it nevertheless does not assume that as a matter of course the subjectivity is all set, as a matter of course has even an actual idea of the significance of this good. This development or remaking of the subjectivity, its infinite concentration in itself under a conception of the infinite's highest good, an eternal happiness, is the developed possibility of the subjectivity's first possibility. . . . (CUP 130)

There we have the basis for the equivocal usage. "Subjectivity" may refer to that initial state of the individual including all of the idiosyncrasies that Kant referred to as "inclinations." It includes, also, the possibility for development in a way that would constitute one's highest good. "Subjectivity" may also refer to that state of the individual in which that highest good is attained, the ideal of the self. The prescription is to divest oneself of subjectivity in the sense that involves giving priority to inclinations and to "transform" oneself in such a way as to be receptive to one's highest good, to become subjective in the second sense. As Kierkegaard wrote, "[B]y subjectivity what one calls a subject should not be understood, but becoming a subject or the developed subjectivity" (P VI B 32).

"Subjectivity," then, refers to the ideal of self, to development of the individual in such as a way as to constitute realization of oneself. That is precisely what we saw Climacus to mean by "truth." "Truth is subjectivity," then, is a tautology. Its titillating sound serves to provoke us to ask what it means and why it might be said, with the possible result that attention would come to rest on the question of what it means to realize oneself as a person. As a bit of indirect communication, it cannot guarantee that result, and the history of criticism concerning it attests to that fact. It is not Kierkegaardian doctrine. Indeed, in the margin of notes for *Postscript*, Kierkegaard wrote, "Paganism culminates in the sentence that truth is subjectivity. Socrates' ignorance is more truth than all pagan knowledge. Inside that sentence is again the Christian truth" (P VI B 40, 26). The statement that the high point of paganism and the truth of Christianity coincide could only make sense if it is a formula that can be supplied content in different ways. To say that truth is manifested in Socratic ignorance is simply to say that the Socratic expression of ignorance is the realization of the highest possibility attainable in paganism. Thus, the prelude that consisted in a critique of views of truth employed in epistemological reflections was not aimed at improvement within that kind of enterprise. It simply provided the starting point for a redirection of concerns—away from the pursuit of knowledge as one's primary task toward concern for one's relationship to an ideal of self. All three of the reasons for seeing Climacus as appealing to the subjectivity of truth as a ploy in the defense of Christianity are, therefore, without merit. The concern of *Fragments* is with truth understood as self-realization, not propositional truth.

Eternity, Immortality, Infinity

The language in which the concern of *Fragments* is articulated is the language of orthodox Christianity, as we saw at the beginning of this chapter. Indeed that is the language of the questions on the title page of *Fragments*, as we saw also. We also saw that is the language used by Climacus to express his concern in the introduction to *Postscript*. "I . . . assume that a highest good called an eternal happiness awaits me" (CUP 15). The question I wish to address here is this: How can that language be reconciled with the response Climacus sees Christianity as providing, which seems as paradoxical as Climacus's words? The concern for acquiring an eternal blessedness is met with the injunction effectively to forget it. The prescription is to imitate Christ, the suffering servant, to take no care for tomorrow. What is apparently desired is well-being that is immune to time, and the prescription would turn one away from even worrying about tomorrow. That would certainly divert attention from the concern, but does it address the concern?

Determining whether or not the response addresses the concern requires attending carefully to what the concern is. I have tried to develop an account of what the concern is. What is needed here is an understanding of the connection between that account and the language that is used to articulate it. We are given a relatively early indication of Climacus's understanding of the language used. He says, "Objectively the question [of immortality] cannot be answered at all, because objectively the question of immortality cannot be asked, since immortality is precisely the intensification and highest development of the developed subjectivity" (CUP 173). The concept of immortality, as Climacus uses it, is not about some extratemporal "matter of fact." Climacus is explicit about this. "The question is asked: how does he, existing, hold on to his consciousness of immortality, lest the metaphysical conception of immortality go and confuse the ethical conception to the point of its becoming an illusion?" (CUP 175).

This is instructive because of the fact that Climacus sees the conceptions of *immortality* and *eternity* to be equivalent. In accordance with his eschewal of the objective approach to the question of immortality, he says that "in a fantastical sense, all systematic thinking is *sub specie aeterni* [under the aspect of eternity] and to that extent immortality is there as eternity. But this immortality is not at all the one inquired about, since the question is about the immortality of a mortal, and that question is not answered by showing that the eternal is immortal, because the eternal is, after all, not the mortal, and the immortality of the eternal is a tautology and a misuse of words" (CUP 171). The comment about the question of immortality is, therefore, a comment about the question about eternity, in the sense that refers to the object of desire of a person. That comment warns us against attributing customary associations with those key concepts employed by Climacus.

A footnote by Climacus is suggestive of considerations that will help to develop a basis for the understanding we are seeking. "Poetry and art," Climacus writes, " have been called an anticipation of the eternal" (CUP 313n.). While Climacus sees that as potentially problematic, an account of why art and poetry might be so called and why it is only anticipatory will be helpful.

Some poets have seen their art as responsive to what is essential in human life. When that view is coupled with the idea that what is essential in human life is a need that is articulated as "longing for eternity," the resulting view is that the concern expressed in *Fragments* can be met through art. Wordsworth and Wallace Stevens provide good examples of the view that the poet is representative of persons in general. According to Stevens, "art sets out to express the human soul."[27] Wordsworth's distaste for so-called "poetic diction" was based on his view that poetry should present what belongs to being human, while "poetic diction" presented the capricious and arbitrary.

> The poet is chiefly distinguished from other men by a greater promptness to think and feel without immediate external excitement, and a greater power in expressing such thoughts and feelings as are produced in him in that manner. But these passions and thoughts and feelings are the general passions and thoughts and feelings of men.[28]

The other part of the view is articulated by Baudelaire. He sees the poet as responsive to the "thirst for the infinite." This is a third expression for what has been called the "longing for eternity" and the "desire for immortality." In accordance with the customary understanding of the key concept involved, Baudelaire sees time as the obstacle to satisfaction of this desire.

The view I attribute to Baudelaire can be pieced together from poems in *Flowers of Evil*, the poem "Intoxication," and essays in *The Poem of Hashish*. Consider the following lines from "To the Reader":

> But among the jackals, panthers, bitches,
> Monkeys, scorpions, vultures, serpents,
> The monsters squealing, yelling, grunting crawling
> In the infamous menagerie of our vices
> There is one uglier, more wicked and more foul than all!
> Although he does not make great gestures or great cries,

---

[27]Wallace Stevens, *The Necessary Angel* (New York: Vintage Books, 1951) 30.

[28]William Wordsworth, "Preface to Lyrical Ballads," *Selected Essays*, ed. Raysor and Raysor, 16.

He would gladly make the earth a shambles
And swallow the world in a yawn:
It is boredome! his eyes weeping an involuntary tear,
He dreams of gibbets as he smokes his hookah.
You know him, reader, this delicate monster,
—Hypocrite reader—my twin—my brother.[29]

If we understand boredom as the felt oppressiveness of time, then it is apparent that time is regarded as an enemy that needs to be overcome. It is also apparent that the effort to overcome that enemy is the pursuit of beauty and/or virtue, since boredom is the epitome of ugliness and wickedness.

Other poems are more explicit about the antagonistic character of time, the function of beauty in combatting it, and about beauty as the inspiration of the poet. In "The Albatross," the poet is likened to a captured albatross on the deck of a ship.

As soon as they have placed them on the deck,
These kings of the sky, awkward and ashamed,
Pitiably let their white wings
Drag at their sides like oars. . . .

And the Poet is like the prince of the clouds,
Who haunts the tempest and mocks the archer;
Exiled on the earth in the midst of derision,
His giant wings keep him from walking.[30]

As an exile on the earth, the poet is outside his natural habitat and time is his enemy. In "The Enemy,"

—O grief! O grief! Time eats away life,
And the dark Enemy who gnaws the heart
Grows and thrives on the blood we lose. (Flowers 31)

An antidote to this mortal enemy is clearly identified in "Hymn to Beauty."

It is of little consequence whether you come from heaven or hell,
O Beauty! huge, terrifying, artless monster!
In your eyes, your smile, your feet open for me the gate
Of an Infinity I love and have never known?

---

[29]Charles Baudelaire, *Flowers of Evil*, ed. and trans. Wallace Fowlie (New York: Bantam Books, 1964) 21.
[30]Baudelaire, *Flowers of Evil*, 25.

From Satan or God, what difference? Angel or Siren,
What difference, if you make—O fairy with soft eyes,
Rhythm, perfume, light, O my one queen—
The universe less hideous and time less heavy?

(Flowers, 41-43)

And it is beauty that inspires the poet, as the poem, "Beauty,"
says.

I am as beautiful, O mortals! as a dream of stone,
And my breast, on which each man is wounded in turn,
Is made to inspire in the poet a love
As eternal and mute as matter. (Flowers, 37)

These poems, then, paint a picture of time as onerous and of
the poet as battling against it. This does not mean that poetry is
seen as the only weapon that can be used. The prose poem
"Intoxication," sums up the view.

You must always be intoxicated. It is the key to all: the one
question. In order not to feel the horrible burden of Time
breaking your back and bending you toward the earth, you must
become drunk, without truce.

But on what? On wine, poetry or virtue, as you wish. But
you must get drunk.

And if at times, on the steps of a palace, on the green grass
of a ditch, in the mournful solitude of your room, you awaken,
and your intoxication is already diminished or gone, ask the
wind, the wave, the star, the bird, the clock, everything that flees,
everything that groans, everything that rolls, that sings, that
speaks, ask what time it is; and the wind, the wave, the star, the
bird, the clock will answer you: "It is time to get intoxicated! In
order not to be slaves martyred by Time, always become
intoxicated! On wine, on poetry or on virtue, as you will."

(Flowers, 149)

Poetry is, thus, seen as one way to obliterate the sense of the
oppressiveness of time and thereby quench the "thirst for the
infinite."

While poetry is seen as only one way of striving for "the
infinite," in *The Poem of Hashish*, the pharmacological approach is
seen as a degraded form of the search. Baudelaire holds this view

despite his belief that "poetry is born, in a mind beset by hash-ish."[31] One brief remark by Baudelaire in his explanation of the immorality of taking hashish, a remark that is almost incidental, may be exploited to see why poetry may be seen as at best anticipatory of the eternal and not an effective route to it.

The experimentation with hashish that provided the occasion for Baudelaire's essays took place among friends in a social setting. Yet, Baudelaire remarks, "Need I add that hashish, like all solitary joys, makes the individual useless to mankind, and society superfluous to the individual" (*Poem*, 116). What makes the experience of hashish a "solitary joy"? What makes it solitary is that it does not grow out of any kind of interaction with others, even if others are present. Nothing emerges from it that generates interaction with others. Unlike the nonpharmacologically induced "poetic vision," no artifact results.

When there is a poem, there is something that represents the person of the poet. To say that a poem is representative in this sense is not to appeal to an expression theory of art. It is to say no more than Wallace Stevens says in calling poetry a "process of the personality of the poet."[32] That does not hold the poem to repre-sent any particular experience or emotion but that the poem grows out of the interaction of the poet with his or her environment. Hence, when the poet's work is heard or read, there is symbolic interaction between the audience and the poet. For one who has the "poetic vision" without creating, the experience remains self-enclosed; the joy is solitary.

It is important to note that the interaction between the poet and his or her audience is only symbolic. There is no actual reciprocity, no mutual giving and taking that develops and weaves around shared experiences. Such communication as there is remains a one-way occurrence. While the pharmacological approach involves no sharing of self with others, the poetic approach involves symbolic sharing. As symbolic sharing of self, poetry intimates a possibility that can be realized not through it

---

[31]Charles Baudelaire, *The Poem of Hashish*, trans. John Githens and Sallie Sullivan (New York: Harper & Row, 1971) 88.

[32]Stevens, *The Necessary Angel*, 45.

but through actually living together. (This incorporates the general view of art advanced by Albert Hofstadter in *Truth and Art*. "In the work of art we are confronted with a symbol which, like all language, articulates human existence, but in particular articulates that mode of human existence which has to do with the search for spiritual truth."[33])

Baudelaire has inadvertently pointed to an understanding of the "thirst for the infinite" that is at odds with his explicit understanding of it as the desire to overcome time. It is that other understanding that coincides with the view I attribute to Climacus. Is there anything in addition to the textual evidence I have adduced that might lead to an understanding of the desire for "the infinite," "immortality," and "eternal blessedness" as the desire for sharing oneself with others?

Of the three expressions used to articulate the desire, two of them explicitly involve negative terms, *infinite* (*not* finite) and *immortal* (*not* mortal). Given the usual understanding of *eternity* as atemporality (state of not being temporal), all three expressions can be seen as articulating a desire for something expressed by a negative concept. The significance of that observation stems from the fact that negative expressions have no definite descriptive force without further ado. They indicate no definite feature of any object, situation, or event. To say that something is not square, for example, fails to assign it any definite shape. It is to say that it is triangular or pentagonal or hexagonal and so on to infinity. Or it may be to say that it is not the kind of thing that has shape. A definite description requires further information. It is *not* square *but* circular, say.

The problem with the usual understanding of the concepts in question is that it takes those concepts to be definitely descriptive. The negated terms, temporality and limitation, are, however, universally applicable to our experience. Kant's reference to time as a form of intuition marks his recognition that all experiences are had as temporal. The very notion of an experience presupposes that experiences are distinguishable, that there are limits marking one experience from another. That being the case, there is nothing

---

[33]Albert Hofstadter, *Truth and Art* (New York: Minerva Press, 1968) 179.

in our experience to which the negated terms would apply, and they are understood as definitely descriptive of some realm beyond the experiences of this world. The expressions used by Climacus and the poets, thus, seem to point to a desire for something beyond human experience.

There is, however, no reason to think that whenever there is a desire, there is some real object that is the object of that desire. It is commonplace to imagine better circumstances than those that prevail and to take steps to bring them about in order to satisfy some desire. Is it the case, though, that whenever there is a desire, there is at least some imagined object that corresponds to the desire? Are desires intentional? There certainly are cases where real work has to be done in order to extract from someone some understanding of what one wants and not because the person was being coy about expressing himself or herself. We can be in the dark about what we want. We can be mistaken about what we want. (That was part of Plato's argument that tyrants lack power. They do not do what they want because they do not know what they really want [*Gorgias* 467a-68e].) What seems to be constant in desire is some sense of the imperfection of the existing state of affairs. That sense may range from acute ("Does this ever hurt!") to extremely mild ("Turn the volume up just a notch, please."). It may range from extremely vague ("I don't know what's the matter.") to definite ("This is the house for me!"). A desire that is expressed in terms of a negative concept falls at the extremely vague end of the spectrum and may run the range from acute to mild. An unhappily married person who wants out of the marriage may have moved from an initial mild sense of dissatisfaction to the point of rage and just wanting out. That person would still have some way to go towards getting what one really wants and the first thing that needs to be done is to formulate some sense of what that is. "Out of the marriage" or "not being in the marriage" is consistent with an infinite number of situations.

Similarly, the desire for the infinite, immortality, eternity is a manifestation of dissatisfaction with human experience. Those negative expressions, however, only articulate a desire to be "out of the marriage." They do not identify exactly what is unsatisfactory in such a way as to point to some definite alternative that is preferable. Just as the unhappily married person needs to determine to some extent what the source of dissatisfaction was in order to increase the probability of satisfactoriness for a subsequent relationship, the object of the desire for the infinite needs to be understood by discerning the source of dissatisfaction. Baudelaire's remarks point to the self-enclosedness of experience as what is unsatisfactory. Poetry (art in general) suggests the possibility of genuine communication, the possibility of living together as in community as the way to negate that unsatisfactory condition. That is what is counselled in the way offered in the un-Socratic alternative considered by Climacus. The example of the Teacher is that of one who is one with is fellowman, who loves others as himself. That is the ideal of community. What is offered as the way to eternal blessedness is, on this analysis, constitutive of it. It is here as with the truth, as Climacus sees it that the *How* constitutes the *What*. Thus, for considerations independent of the text, the view ascribed to the text can be seen as tenable. Climacus's insistence that he is not engaged in metaphysics is not just a dodge to avoid questionable metaphysical implications of his view.

The limited claim on behalf of poetry, the claim that poetry is an "anticipation of the eternal," represents a triumph over the more ambitious claim that had a home in Romanticism, namely that art can deliver the eternal. Art, on the view of Climacus, can only point to the possibility, which cannot be realized aesthetically. It takes real life—that is, real life, not imagined life.

Chapter 4
The Ethics of Persuasion

Kierkegaard's comment on the misunderstanding of the reviewer of *Fragments* shows his awareness of the failure of his efforts at indirect communication in important places. His overt attacks on the Church of Denmark in *The Moment* during his later years also attest to his awareness of his ineffectiveness. This perceived failure does not settle the question of the practical justification for indirect communication. It is, of course, conceivable that the efforts were successful in some quarters. That success would not be a matter of public record, since it would consist in some inward transformation. Even if the efforts did not result in undetected successes, they might still have been practically justifiable for the reasons developed in the first chapter.

Objections to Direct Persuasion

The case for the practical justifiability of indirect communication is distinct from the ethical justification for indirect communication. It might be argued that while Kierkegaard is right in thinking that there is an ethical requirement to respect the autonomy of his audience, that principle does not *require* indirect communication. After all, people try to persuade other people about all sorts of things all of the time without any sense that moral scruples would indicate that there is anything wrong with that. Indeed there are religious proselytizers and, specifically, promoters or Christianity all over the globe. The notion that respect for autonomy would require indirect communication suggests that there is something wrong with such direct persuasive efforts. What could be the basis for such thinking?

We can imagine trying to persuade a young person to pursue a higher education. Such an effort on our part may be considered laudable. We are, after all, familiar with the ways of the world in the way that a young person may not be, and we would be sharing in our wisdom. The aim would be to have the young person put himself/herself in position to take advantage of opportunities that would not be available without a higher education. We would have potentially contributed to the young person's ability to realize himself/herself in ways that one otherwise never would have dreamed. This kind of effort recognizes the autonomy of the other while also recognizing that the environment in which one finds oneself may inhibit or enhance self-realization, and the effort aims at getting the young person into an environment that would be self-enhancing. There seems to be nothing ethically objectionable about direct persuasive communication in cases of this sort.

The case is not so clear with respect to promoting a particular place of higher education. If the person has expressed an interest in a technical education, it would certainly be permissible to provide information about candidate institutions. It would also be permissible to provide an account of how a liberal education would be beneficial to a person who wanted to specialize in a technical area. What would be the justification, though, for advocating one school over another? Is that not to interfere in an area of choice that is appropriately left alone? It begins to look more like efforts to control a life than like efforts to enable a person to make his/her own life. That makes it ethically suspect.

The situation becomes even more suspicious if we attempt to convince someone to choose a particular major or to follow a certain career path. What could be the justification for advocacy in those areas? There would be nothing wrong with providing information about the advantages and disadvantages of various career paths. That would be a matter of imparting knowledge, and Kierkegaard would agree that direct communication of knowledge is appropriate. Choosing a career path is a different matter from taking in information about possibilities, however. It would, indeed, be presumptuous for one person to suppose that one was in a position to say what the appropriate career would be for another. It would be presumptuous, because the supposition involved is the supposition of superiority with respect to an understanding of what would constitute a satisfactory professional life for another. One person cannot presume to know what would provide a sense of professional fulfillment for another person. There are alternatives available, and what suits one person may not suit another.

The Ideal of Personhood

Is it the case that we suppose that there are alternative ways of realizing oneself as person? That is, do we suppose that just as there are alternative satisfactory ways of realizing professional aspirations there are also alternative satisfactory fundamental life principles such that one would do just as well as another? If it is the case that there are alternative satisfactory life principles, then, just as with career choices, it would be presumptuous for one person to suppose that one knows what would be appropriate for another.

Do we suppose, rather, that there is *an* ideal of personhood, not alternative ideals? That is the view with which Kierkegaard operates, as we have seen. On the assumption of a single ideal of personhood, one person certainly *would* know what it would take for another person to realize himself/herself as a person. The supposed unwarranted assumption, therefore, would have to be that the other person does not know the ideal or that the other person does not know that his/her relationship to the ideal is deficient. Why would those assumptions be seen as unwarranted? Alternatively put: (1)What is the basis for the assumption that everyone knows the Ethical? (2) What is the basis for thinking that one person cannot say where another stands in relation to the Ethical?

(1) The One Ideal Assumption

Let us view the matter first from a Kierkegaardian perspective and recall that the assumption in question is the same as the view that the Socratic expresses the proper relationship between two persons. That is to say that one person stands in the same relationship to the Truth as another. It is for that reason that one person cannot be in a position of authority with respect to the Ethical. According to the analysis in *Fragments*, that is the case prior to the Teacher's providing the Truth and after the Teacher's appearance. "[O]nce the condition is given, that which was valid for the Socratic is again valid" (PF 63). How is it, though, that the relationship of equality is constituted prior to the Teacher's providing the Truth?

The acquiring of the Truth is understood as a breach with immanence. The breach with immanence is a break with the idea of man in the natural stance. According to *Fragments*, what is miraculous, what is unintelligible is precisely the notion of a possibility that did not derive from antecedent conditions. This is the anti-Hegelian position that is suggested in the opening line of *Either/Or* I. "It may at times have occurred to you, dear reader, to doubt somewhat the accuracy of that familiar philosophical thesis that the outer is the inner and the inner is the outer" (EOI 3). Kierkegaard's position is that both prior to and after the breach, everyone is in a position of equality. Why? If we follow the Biblical line, man was created in the divine image, that is, with the Truth. Nothing separates man from the divine until the Fall. With the Fall, no one is in the right relationship with God; no one has the Truth. Insofar as no one is in the right relationship, no one has a basis for claiming superiority to any other. With the coming of the Teacher, everyone has the possibility of restoration of the right relationship. Thus, before and after, there is equality.

If we do not follow the Biblical line and we understand the Ethical ideal as natural, that still places each individual in the same essential relationship to it. The notion of the ethical ideal as natural encompasses a number of different ways of understanding in what the Ethical consists. We may think of the desire for standing in the eyes of others as the source of an understanding of the ethical ideal. That view yields the Homeric notion of *arete* as honor. The one who exhibits the qualities that allow one to prevail in war and competition is hailed as a real man. The capacity to behave in the honored ways is something that is natural and available to all. If not, the defining feature of humanity would be something that is absent in some humans, and that is an unintelligible notion.

If the understanding of what it is to be a person is broadened to include our relationship to a larger whole, our view of what it takes to prevail in behavior that is seen as constituting the height of human possibility changes. While on this view the ethical ideal is now understood as essentially related to the well-being of the group, that does not mark some radical departure (breach) from the prior understanding. It is simply a matter of coming to see our well-being as individuals as not capable of being secured by solitary pursuits.[1] Hegel chronicled the growth of this idea from the family to the state in *Philosophy of Right*. The special connection between the idea of the Ethical and rationality in philosophy is, no doubt, in part attributable to the role of reason in assessing the relationship between the good of the whole and individual conduct and in devising rules for securing a positive relationship. Societal institutions that govern our lives are the repositories of the wisdom of the ages, as it were. Kierkegaard's use of this understanding is clear in *Fear and Trembling*, in which the Abraham-Isaac relationship, a familial connection, is used to represent the highest ethical relationship, and explicit reference is made to Hegel (p. 83) in the view of the ethical as constituting the universal-human. The notion that there is a requirement of some sort that calls for breaking with the ethical is called absurd. It defies reason. This shows the connection that is presupposed between the Ethical and the rational. Additionally, we are aware of Kant's understanding of reason and will as the ground of the fundamental ethical imperative. We are speaking here of what is understood as defining a person. Thus, when the ethical is understood as grounded in nature, whether that nature is understood as some nonrational or rational aspect of ourselves, we are all understood as participating

---

[1]Interestingly, the story of the development of this view, as told by Plato's *Protagoras*, does involve divine intervention in human affairs to impart to all the virtue of justice as the condition for civil society (*Protagoras* 320c-322d). The prior understanding was not as atomistic as may be suggested by "solitary pursuits," but there was a decidedly more restricted view of whose honor was governing. Thus, while Achilles was certainly motivated by his own personal honor, as was Agamemnon, both were involved in a corporate effort. To be sure, that corporate effort was inspired by a dignitary affront to a single individual, but that individual was someone other than King Agamemnon. It was his brother, Menelaus, with whose wife, Helen, Paris had absconded. The enlargement of the idea of whose welfare appropriately claimed one's allegiance is represented in the Oresteian trilogy. There it is shown how the narrowly focussed attention to honor yields interminable conflict. The goddess Athena blesses the idea of civic virtue as triumphing over narrower concerns. This representation, as in *Protagoras*, sees the emergence of this broader the idea of the ethical as natural. To see the gods as implanting it or sanctioning it is to see it as natural.

in it. There can be no superiority of one person over another in that respect. That is Kierkegaard's view.

Is Kierkegaard right about this, though? He offers no argument for the view; he simply operates with it. The thesis that there is a singular ideal of person is advanced and defended by James N. Loughran.

> I am claiming that all "normally formed" human beings, in virtue of their "personalness," have dispositions for rationality, freedom, love, self-respect, and the rest; these are the capacities they want to activate and exercise; these are the goods they want to realize. Not "should want"; "want!" My claim is a factual claim. And my evidence is the same sort of evidence offered by Becker [Lawrence Becker, *On Justifying Moral Judgments*] (and, indeed, Gewirth [Alan Gewirth, *Reason and Morality*]) in his starker, to say the least, description of species-wide features of human beings: my knowledge of myself and others around me as well as what I have learned in general—from literature, the arts, history, the social and natural sciences—of the aspirations, motivations, evaluations, successes, failures, etc., etc. of men and women. Clearly I am not claiming privileged knowledge or evidence available only to me; rather I claim that you too already have this knowledge, based on similar evidence.[2]

Loughran is right to put the word "normally formed" in quotation marks, because it surely cries out for consideration of question begging. Without focussing on the loaded word, Loughran does explicitly address the matter of question begging. He gives us three considerations as evidence for the fact of the authority of the ideal in our lives: (a) our sense "that things like murder, torture, rape, lying, breaking promises, etc. are wrong." (b) "our spontaneous and firm feelings of approval for men and women who are benevolent, fair, honest, faithful, etc. . . . [And our] disapproval for those who are malevolent, unfair, dishonest, unfaithful, etc." (c) "our concern to show a particular public image" as evidence that we are "rightly judged."[3]

It is important to note the force of the three considerations. The first two would be persuasive to those who admit to sharing in the

---

[2]James N. Loughran, "The Moral Ideal of the Person," *International Philosophical Quarterly* 26/2 (June 1986): 153.

[3]Ibid., 156.

dispositions described and whose associates are such as to share in those dispositions with respect to themselves and those they know. The third one aims at persuading us with respect to the vast majority of people whom we do not know. It is, however, question begging, for it imputes to those people precisely the disposition that Loughran wants to show that they have, namely, acceptance of the ideal. All Loughran has a right to claim on the basis of the public behavior of others is that they know that they are judged by the ideal, not that they are *rightly* judged. Antiphon cannot simply be dismissed. "[J]ustice consists in not transgressing the laws and usages (nomia) of one's state. Therefore the most profitable means of manipulating justice is to respect the laws when witnesses are present but otherwise to follow the precepts of nature."[4]

In response to the challenge to his position that appeals to the fact of what might be called moral monsters, Loughran makes an additional argument that is obviously question begging. "I handle the 'moral monster' objection as Becker would: such individuals are not 'normally formed.' "[5] The thesis is, after all, that "normally formed" individuals accept the moral ideal of a person. If someone points to someone who does not accept the ideal, the response that such a person is not normally formed obviously begs the question.

These observations about the presumed targets of Loughran's arguments inspire a question about the point of arguments of the sort made by Loughran. Who might be convinced? If Loughran is right, then either (a) his audience is such that it accepts and acknowledges the ideal or (b) it accepts and does not acknowledge the ideal. By "acceptance of the ideal" I refer to Loughran's thesis that "human beings are at least implicitly aware of and drawn to a multifaceted ideal of the person; they recognize its authoritative status and want to realize it in their lives."[6] By "acknowledging the ideal" I mean explicit awareness of the ideal such that its fundamental status is recognized in moral reasoning and/or efforts are made to conform one's conduct to its requirements because of its authoritative status. If the former is the case (a), the argument is

---

[4]W. K. C. Guthrie, *The Sophists* (Cambridge UK: Cambridge University Press, 1971) 108.

[5]Loughran, "The Moral Ideal of the Person," 156.

[6]Ibid., 154.

not needed.[7] If the latter is the case (b), then there is some schism in the self, and we would need to ask whether or not such is schism is due to some intellectual consideration that could be bridged by argument.

Why might one not acknowledge an ideal that one accepts? The fact of nonacknowledgement of the ideal one accepts is indeed one of the ideas used by Loughran to respond to the challenge that appeals to the fact that people behave in ways that are inconsistent with the demands of the ideal. "Sometimes they lose sight of this ideal or are confused about what, say, freedom, love, or self-respect really mean."[8] It is important to note that there are two possible explanations here, not one with an alternative locution added. The two are (1) refusal to acknowledge something and (2) conceptual confusion. Failure to conform one's conduct to the demands of the ideal may be the result of refusal to acknowledge the authority of the ideal or it may be the result of misunderstanding about what that ideal requires. The latter is not a case in which any argument about the fundamental status of the ideal is relevant. The former, referred to by the metaphor of "losing sight of the ideal" needs to be examined in order to determine if it could be remedied by argument.

The matter of "losing sight of the ideal" can be understood as episodic or as systematic. That is, one could be thought of as losing sight of the ideal in some act that can be seen as a momentary lapse. That is the sort of phenomenon that philosophers generally discuss under the rubric of *akrasia* or moral weakness. That is not at issue here, because for an act to be understood as one of moral weakness, the standard from which it is a deviation needs to be acknowledged. The question in that case is: How do you account for a person's failure to conform to an ideal that one accepts and acknowledges? Consequently, "losing sight of the ideal" here must be understood as some sustained position, in which failure to

---

[7]The argument would not be needed to induce the person in question to govern his/her life according to the ideal or to use it in moral reasoning. It could make a difference in that person's efforts to be persuasive to others, however, since acceptance and acknowledgement of the ideal does not entail the belief that others accept the ideal as well.

[8]Ibid., 154.

conform to the demands of the ideal is ongoing, and that failure is not simply a matter of conceptual confusion.

Imagine a life, then, that is driven by narrow self-interest, whether that self-interest is understood as the pursuit of material goods, power, or pleasure, and in which concern for others enters decision making principally as a pragmatic matter or, in any case, as a secondary consideration. According to Loughran, the systematic deviation from the demands of the ideal, the "loss of sight of the ideal," is a result of the failure to acknowledge what one, in fact, accepts. How could that occur? That could occur if there are competing norms of behavior, norms which are given some societal sanction, even if they are not explicitly offered as ideals.

Indeed, there *are* competing images of personhood in our world. In addition to the representation of Loughran's ideal in parental modelling and counselling and in a number of public and private institutions (schools, civic, and religious organizations), we are bathed in a sea of commercially driven images which portray the attainment of fulfillment as, say, finally being alone in a Honda or comfortably cached with beauties and beer. The systematic victory of the commercially driven norm would mean, according to Loughran's thesis, that a person is in rebellion against himself/herself. Rebellion against oneself is not a matter of suffering from some cognitive defect that can be rectified by argument. If it were, therapists would need to function as philosophers in order to have any kind of success. That is, what would be needed to assist people who are at odds with themselves in the fundamental way discussed here would be a logical and epistemological enterprise. Clearly, that is not the way of therapy. What is more, the thesis sees the acceptance of the ideal that is not acknowledged as occurring at some prereflective level. Since argument aims at attention to the reflective level, it effectively presupposes that the schism is some kind of cognitive defect. Since it is not, however, argument cannot remove it, and Loughran's argumentative effort to establish his thesis cannot work. After all, Loughran aims at convincing his audience to acknowledge the authority of the ideal he describes. Indeed, we would be surprised if anyone thought that by argument someone was either changed into a good person or was changed in his/her explicit understanding of what makes for a good person.

My attempt to explain a fact that we must acknowledge, namely, that there are persons whose lives appear to exhibit systematic
deviation from the ideal of love, appealed to the fact that there are
clearly different images of the "successful" person that operate in
our world. Loughran's arguments for the universal acceptance of
the ideal of love are not convincing. The ideal is a fundamental
principle, and its governance of an entire life means that there is
no activity that falls outside it that might be made the basis for
pragmatic justification for it.[9] This means that one of the assumptions on which the ethical barrier to direct communication of the
Ethical rested, namely, that there is a single ideal that everyone
knows, cannot be established. That was the assumption that led to
the idea of equality with respect to the Ethical, such that one person's assumption of superiority would be presumptuous. In the absence of any finding of equality with respect to the Ethical, the
ethical requirement of indirect communication cannot be established.

My argument need not apply to Kierkegaard, however. His
world was far more homogeneous than ours. The varied vehicles
that we have (mass media) that communicate to children the sense
of what it is to be a person were simply nonexistent. What is more,
it was an officially Christian state. It would have been reasonable
(in any case, a lot more reasonable than for us) for Kierkegaard to
assume, then, that there was a single ideal that was given societal
sanction.

Let us suppose, then, that Kierkegaard is right about that. Does
it follow, as he would have it, that no one may direct or instruct
(directly communicate) another to realize what everyone has the
potential to realize? The reasoning is that since everyone equally
has the potential, no one is in a position of authority, and if no one
is in a position of authority, no one may direct or instruct another.
This argument is reminiscent of one made in *Protagoras* about
whether or not virtue can be taught. Socrates argues that unlike
matters in which there is technical expertise, debate in the
Assembly about matters of governance is not restricted to those

---

[9]See Benjamin Daise, "The Will to Truth in Kierkegaard's Philosophical
Fragments," *Philosophy of Religion* 31:1-12.

who are recognized authorities. "The reason must be that they [the Athenians] do not think that this is a subject that can be taught" (*Protagoras* 319d). This argument might be extended to come closer to the one Kierkegaard makes. If there is a matter about which it is impossible for one person to be an authority, it is impermissible for someone to behave as if one were an authority. Presuming to direct or instruct someone to realize himself/herself as a person is behaving as if one were an authority.

Protagoras's response to Socrates is suggestive of a response to Kierkegaard. Protagoras says that the fact that there is no special group of authorities on matters of governance does not mean that there is no one with authority, but that all have authority. "But when the subject of their counsel involves political wisdom . . . they listen to everyman's opinion, for they think that everyone must share in this kind of virtue" (*Protagoras* 322e). The argument is that since everyone is equally equipped with the potentiality, everyone is, in principle, able to direct and instruct. That response would remove Kierkegaard's ability to infer the *impermissibility* of purporting to direct and instruct from the *inability* to direct and instruct, because it would remove the claim of inability. Indeed, this is Kierkegaard's view, insofar as he says that everyone knows the Ethical. The Socratic argument in *Protagoras* is not one that Kierkegaard would make.[10]

(2)Assuming the Defiance of Another

Is there some other reason it might be thought that given essential equality with respect to the Ethical it would be ethically impermissible for one person to direct or instruct another? It may be that the posture from which one proposes to direct or instruct another presupposes that one knows that the other is in need of instruction or direction, and it may be that presupposition that is ethically indefensible. One might be thought to need direction or instruction because (a) one is confused about one's relationship to

---

[10]For the record, the argument against the teachability of virtue is not one that Socrates makes on his own behalf. The account that he gives is in terms of what the Athenians do and what the Athenians believe (*Protagoras* 322d-323d). So the conclusion he draws is one he purports to be implicitly held by the Athenians.

the requirements of the Ethical (b) one is in defiance of the requirements of the Ethical, the claim of which one accepts on some level.

(a) Might it be that the view that someone is confused about
one's relationship to the requirements of the Ethical is subject to
the charge of presumptuousness? That charge cannot be sustained.
Confusion may be manifested in the words that one uses to articulate one's understanding of the Ethical. This is clearly exemplified
in the depiction of his contemporaries by Johannes de Silentio in
Fear and Trembling.

Praising Abraham as the Father of Faith while trumpeting the
Hegelianism that views faith as a primitive form of the relationship
to the Absolute is rightly seen as involving a confusion about what
faith is and, hence, about what might be required by faith. There
is nothing presumptuous in noting that—in directly noting that.
Noting the confusion presupposes some cognitive superiority, but
inasmuch as cognitive superiority (which may be case-specific) is
not superiority as a person, there is nothing ethically offensive
about presupposing it. That being the case, the use of indirect
communication in that connection may be pragmatically required
but not ethically required.

(b) Might it be that the assumption that one knows that
another person is in defiance of the Ethical is subject to the charge
of presumptuousness? Insofar as whether or not one is being
defiant is determined by one's internal disposition, the assumption
that one person knows how another stands in relationship to the
Ethical is indeed presumptuous. To say this is not to say that we
do not appropriately make judgments about the motivations, the
moods, the emotional states of others. We cannot avoid making
those kinds of judgments in the course of our daily dealings with
others. Indeed, some of those judgments are ones we must make
if we are to be sensitive to the concerns of others. So the view
expressed here is not one that claims that a person has special
exclusive access to his/her mental state. Rather, it is the recognition that a specific act may stem from different fundamental
orientations towards the Ethical. This is what is recognized by
Kant's distinction between acting from duty and acting in accordance with duty. The other side of the same kind of coin is
recognized by de Silentio when he proclaims "how monstrous a
paradox faith is, a paradox capable of making a murder into a holy

act well pleasing to God" (FT 82). What is apparently contrary to what one ought to do may be, by virtue of one's relationship to the ideal, precisely what one ought to do. Thus, someone cannot read from the specific act itself just what the relationship of the agent to the ideal is. If that is the case, the presumption that someone is in defiance of the Ethical is presumptuousness.

Suppose someone had the idea that while most of us are rhetorically committed to the idea of equality, many of us are not existentially committed to it, that is, that many of us are in defiance. That is to say, someone might think that while we proclaim that America is the land of equal opportunity and that a person's lot is fundamentally determined by his/her making use of opportunities that are available to all, many of us to do not treat others as equals, and that inequality in our treatment of others is at odds with what we profess. This is not about what happens with people in the context of public and social institutions. This is about how people are in their personal intercourse with each other. Does anyone have standing to assert that there is the kind of discrepancy just described? Entertaining the suspicion is one thing; asserting the fact is quite another. What conditions would have to be met for someone to be justified in making the assertion? The question is here not just about judging any particular act, but an entire orientation in life.

The distinction that is being invoked here—between being conceptually confused, that is confused about the demands of the Ethical, and being in defiance of the Ethical requires some attention. It would be putting the matter too strongly to speak of the phenomenon as "willful disregard," because what is involved may be seen as a form of self-deception. There are various versions of the story of a member of Group A standing before an audience of A and decrying the excesses of Group B. Group A chants, "Amen!" Then the member decries the excesses of Group C, and the audience again intones, "Amen!" The member then says that they should look at some specific actions of Group A. The audience, then, murmurs that "he's stopped preaching and gone to meddling." The point, of course, is that there is no problem in seeing the relationship between specific behaviors and the ideal. Rather, it is in seeing that there is some deficiency in one's own relationship to the ideal, and injection of another's view is seen as inappropriate. The commentator is likely to be seen as a 'holier than thou' sort. Indeed, Group A would be right. Even though the commentator is modest enough to see himself as included in the category of those subject to judgment, he would still have placed himself in the morally superior position of acknowledging his errors, while seeing the others as in need of looking at themselves. It is conceivable that the group might be right in saying to the member-critic that perhaps his conduct stemmed from baser considerations, but theirs stemmed from the loftiest of ideals.

I am not saying that the conceivability of this response is evidence for the correctness of the response. Rather, it points to the question of what evidence the member-critic could have for his judgment. It may be that as a member of the group, he has engaged in conversations with other members such that he can rightly infer something about the basis of their conduct. A witness to racist or sexist private utterances may justifiably impute motives to someone who behaves in a way that slights someone of a different race or sex.

That is not the situation of an author who directs remarks to a public with which one has not had the kind of personal contact that would ground a judgment about motive. The judgment that some unknown member of the reading public stands in a defiant relationship with the ideal and needs to engage in self-reflection would be presumptuous. The morally appropriate way to engage the attention of someone who might need to be jolted is through the Socratic art. Whatever other considerations Kierkegaard may have made, insofar as there was a singular shared ideal, he would be right about the moral requirement of indirect communication. The audience to which Kierkegaard directed his work professed to be Christians. Thus, there was the singular shared ideal. Hence there was an ethical requirement for indirect communication.

Conclusion

What we have seen is that indirect communication is in some sense like pointing. In pointing, the one doing the pointing sees something that the other person does not see and tries to direct the attention of the other to the object so that the other may see for himself. Pointing differs from asserting that there is such and such an object. Asserting does not assist the other in acquiring the information for himself. Acceptance of the assertion rests on acceptance of the authority of the one doing the asserting or the authority of any evidentiary considerations accompanying the assertion. Pointing seeks to engage the other; asserting is unmindful of the possible passivity of the other.

Indirect communication is unlike literal pointing insofar as pointing essentially seeks to engage the other cognitively. Pointing aims at getting the other to see that some part of the world is thus and so. (Of course there are circumstances in which it is already understood that one is to act and the pointing identifies the locus of the action. That is the case when one points to a door to be entered or a person to be summoned.) Success in pointing has as its consequence the other's knowing-that something is the case. Depending on what the object of pointing is, knowing-that may be followed by any attitude ranging from indifference ("Who cares that the sun is just above the horizon?") to immediate action ("I'm out of here!)" Indirect communication aims at making the attitude of indifference impossible by engaging the other in an essentially noncognitive way.

Indirect communication is like pointing that is dynamic, such as when a director points to an actor and then points to a spot. The difference with indirect communication is that the spot is a possibility. Hence, moving to the spot would consist in doing something to realize the possibility. Just as an actor may be inattentive and miss the pointing or see the pointing but fail to see that it is in his direction, so indirect communication may fail because of peculiarities of the target audience. In no communicative effort is success guaranteed.

In literal pointing, if the potential viewer is not inclined to look, artifice may be required to get his attention. Something would need to be done to bring the potential viewer and the pointer into the same realm. A nudge or some attention-getting sound might do the trick. With indirect communication, the artifice consists in artistic creation. That is, there is the making and presentation of a possibility. That possibility needs to be constructed and presented in such a way that there is a bridge erected between it and the world of the audience. Otherwise, it would be like pointing with the pointer at the back of the head of the would-be viewer. Thus, it needs to be ostensibly about something that already matters to the audience, though it need not be ultimately about something that would immediately engage the attention of the audience.

We saw that just as Plato's Socrates assumed a position inside the world of contemporary Athens in order to intimate a path to some clarity about virtue, Kierkegaard used pseudonymity (among other devices) to chart positions inside the world of nineteenth century Danish philosophers and theologians. What we see in Kierkegaard's pseudonymous works is a view from inside the target audience along with bridges to the possibility of acceptance of Christianity. Thus, what Climacus says does not represent simply anybody's view of Christianity. It represents a nineteenth century Danish view with aspects framed in such a way as to constitute hints about alterations that would take one away from the prevailing conceits and deceits.

Kierkegaard's art required, then, a considerable amount of empathy. Kierkegaard had to feel and think himself into the stance of his audience in order to be able to depict that stance through the self-articulation of his pseudonyms. It required a considerable amount of self-giving to be respectful of the freedom of the audience, which is a condition for the decision to act on the possibility presented. In short, even the pseudonymous works are works of love. How appropriate that it would be through such works of love that the effort is made to induce others to entertain the possibility of a life of love!

Bibliography

Kierkegaard's Works

Kierkegaard, Søren. *Concluding Unscientific Postscript*. Two volumes. Translated by Howard V. Hong and Edna H. Hong. Princeton NJ: Princeton University Press, 1992.

_____. *Either/Or*. Two volumes. Translated by Howard V. Hong and Edna H. Hong. Princeton NJ: Princeton University Press, 1987.

_____. *Fear and Trembling*. Translated by Howard V. Hong and Edna H. Hong. Princeton NJ: Princeton University Press, 1983.

_____. *Papirer*. Thirteen volumes. København: Gyldendal, 1968.

_____. *Philosophical Fragments*. Translated by Howard V. Hong and Edna H. Hong. Princeton NJ: Princeton University Press, 1985.

_____. *Samlede Værker*. Twenty volumes. København: Gyldendal, 1963.

_____. *Sickness unto Death*. Translated by Howard V. Hong and Edna H. Hong. Princeton NJ: Princeton University Press, 1980.

Other Works Cited

Aristotle. *The Basic Works of Aristotle*. Edited by Richard McKeon. New York: Random House, 1941.

_____. *Metaphysics*. Translated by Richard Hope. Ann Arbor: University of Michigan Press, 1963.

Baudelaire, Charles. *Flowers of Evil*. Edited and translated by Wallace Fowlie. New York: Bantam Books, 1964.

_____. *The Poem of Hashish*. Translated by John Githens and Sallie Sullivan. New York: Harper & Row, 1971.

Bedu-Addo, J. T. "Recollection and the Argument from a Hypothesis in Plato's *Meno*." *Journal of Hellenic Studies* 104 (1984).

Bluck, R. S. *Plato's Meno*. Cambridge: Cambridge University Press, 1961.

Bouwsma, O. K. "Anselm's Argument." In *Without Proof or Evidence: Essays of O. K. Bouwsma.* Edited by J. L. Craft and R. E. Hustwit. Lincoln: University of Nebraska Press, 1984.

Brumbaugh, R. S. "Plato's *Meno* as Form and as Content of Secondary School Courses in Philosophy." *Teaching Philosophy* 1/2 (Fall 1975).

Daise, Benjamin. "Kierkegaard and the Absolute Paradox." *The Journal of the History of Philosophy* 14/1 (January 1976).

_____. "The Will to Truth in Kierkegaard's Philosophical Fragments." *Philosophy of Religion* (January 1992).

Devereux, Daniel. "Nature and Teaching in Plato's *Meno.*" *Phronesis* 23/2 (1978).

Edwards, Paul. "Kierkegaard and the Truth of Christianity." *Philosophy* 46/176 (April 1971).

Evans, C. Stephen. *Kierkegaard's "Fragments" and "Postscript": The Religious Philosophy of Johannes Climacus.* Atlantic Highlands NJ: Humanities Press, 1983.

_____. *Passionate Reason: Making Sense of Kierkegaard's "Philosophical Fragments."* Bloomington: Indiana University Press, 1992.

_____. "Kierkegaard and Plantinga on Belief in God: Subjectivity as the Ground of Properly Basic Religious Beliefs." *Faith and Philosophy* 5/1 (1988).

Feuerbach, Ludwig. *The Essence of Christianity.* Translated by George Eliot. New York: Harper & Row Publishers, 1957.

Greve, Wilfried. "Against Authority: Abraham in Kierkegaard Research." A paper presented at the International Kierkegaard Conference, St. Olaf College, 11 June 1997.

Guthrie, W. K. C. *The Sophists.* Cambridge UK: Cambridge University Press, 1971.

Hofstadter, Albert. *Truth and Art.* New York: Minerva Press, 1968.

Joint Association of Classics Teachers. *The World of Athens: An Introduction to Classical Athenian Culture.* Cambridge: Cambridge University Press, 1984.

Johnson, Ralph. *The Concept of Existence in Concluding Unscientific Postscript.* The Hague: Martinus Nijhoff, 1972.

Kahn, Charles. "The Greek Verb 'to be' and the Concept of Being." *Foundations of Language.* 1966.

_____. "The Thesis of Parmenides." *The Review of Metaphysics* 22.

Kant, Immanuel. *The Critique of Pure Reason*. Translated by Norman Kemp Smith. New York: St. Martins, 1929.

Kirmmse, Bruce. *Kierkegaard in Golden Age Denmark*. Bloomington: Indiana University Press, 1990.

Kripke, Saul A. *Naming And Necessity*. Cambridge MA: Harvard University Press, 1980.

Loughran, James N. S.J. "The Moral Ideal of the Person." *International Philosophical Quarterly* 26/2 (June 1986).

Lübcke, Poul. "Kierkegaard and Indirect Communication." *History of European Ideas* 12/1 (1990).

Mackey, Louis. *Kierkegaard: A Kind of Poet*. Philadelphia: University of Pennsylvania Press, 1971.

McKinnon, Alastair. *The Kierkegaard Indices*. Volume 2. *Fundamental Polyglot Konkordans Til Kierkegaards Samlede Værker*. Leiden: E. J. Brill, 1971.

Pascal. *Pensées*. Translated by W. F. Trotter. New York: E. P. Dutton, 1958.

Peirce, Charles Sanders. *Collected Papers*. Volumes 5-6. Edited by Charles Hartshorne and P. Weiss. Cambridge MA: Belknap Press of Harvard University Press, 1965.

Plato. *The Collected Dialogues of Plato*. Edited by Edith Hamilton and Huntington Cairns. Princeton NJ: Princeton University Press, 1961.

_____. *Protagoras and Meno*. Translated by W. K. C. Guthrie. London: Penguin Books, 1956.

_____. *Republic*. Translated by G. M. A. Grube and C. D. C. Reeve. Indianapolis: Hackett Publishing Co. Inc., 1992.

Pojman, Louis. *The Logic of Subjectivity*. University AL: University of Alabama Press, 1984.

Popkin, Richard. "Kierkegaard and Skepticism." In *Kierkegaard: A Collection of Critical Essays*. Edited by Josiah Thompson. Garden City NY: Doubleday, 1972.

Quine, W. V. O. *The Ways of Paradox*. New York: Random House, 1968.

Robinson, Richard. *Plato's Earlier Dialectic*. Ithaca NY: Cornell University Press, 1941.

Sprague, Rosamond Kent, editor. *The Older Sophists*. Columbia: University of South Carolina Press, 1972.

Stevens, Wallace. *The Necessary Angel*. New York: Vintage Books, 1951.

Strawser, Michael. *Both/And: Reading Kierkegaard from Irony to Edification*. New York: Fordham University Press, 1997.

Stump, Eleonore, and Norman Kretzmann. "Eternity." *Journal of Philosophy* 78/8 (August 1981).

Søe, N. H. "Kierkegaard's Doctrine of the Paradox." In *A Kierkegaard Critique*. Edited by H. Johnsson and N. Thulstrup. Chicago: Henry Regnery, 1962.

Versényi, Laszlo. "Protagoras' Man-Measure Fragment." *American Journal of Philology* 83 (1962).

Vidal, Gore, and Louis Auchincloss. "Letters: Just Between Cousins." In *The New Yorker* 73/15 (9 June 1997).

Welbourne, Michael. "Meno's Paradox." *Philosophy* 61 (1986).

Wittgenstein, Ludwig. *Tractatus logico-philosophicus*. Translated by D. F. Pears and B. F. McGuinness. London: Routledge & Kegan Paul, 1961.

Whittaker, John. "Kierkegaard on Names, Concepts, and Proofs for God's Existence." *International Journal for the Philosophy of Religion* 10 (1979).

Wordsworth, William. "Preface to Lyrical Ballads." In *Selected Essays*. Edited by Raysor and Raysor.

Zyskind, Harold, R. Sternfeld. "Plato's *Meno* 89c: 'Virtue is Knowledge,' a Hypothesis?" *Phronesis* 21/2.

Index

Kierkegaard's Socratic Art.
by Benjamin Daise.

Mercer University Press, Macon, Georgia 31210-3960.
Isbn 0-86554-655-X (perfectbound). Pick number: MUP/P195.
Text and interior designs and composition by Edmon L. Rowell, Jr.
Cover design by Jim Burt.
Camera-ready pages (x+135) composed on a Gateway2000 386/33C
    and on an AOpen BG45-AP5VM via dos WordPerfect 5.1 and WP
    for Windows 5.1/5.2, and printed on a LaserMaster 1000.
Text fonts: Palatino (Linotype AG via Adobe Type Manager) 11/13.
Display fonts (headings): Palatino.
Printed and bound by McNaughton & Gunn, Saline MI 48176-0010
    via offset lithography on 55# Writers Natural (360ppi).
Trimmed and notchbound into 10-pt. cls covers printed
    2 PMS colors and with layflat matte film lamination.
                                          [1M November 1999]

111099elr